MathFlare

Name: ______________________________

Class: ___________

Teacher: ______________________________

Introduction

As parents and educators, we recognize the pivotal role mathematics plays in shaping a child's academic journey and future success. Yet, the path to mathematical proficiency can often seem daunting, fraught with challenges and complexities. That's where the transformative power of MathFlare Workbooks shine through, illuminating the way forward with clarity, precision, and purpose.

Introducing MathFlare Workbooks – a beacon of guidance, a testament to excellence, and a catalyst for achievement. Crafted with meticulous care and expertise, MathFlare Workbooks stand as paragons of educational excellence, designed to nurture young minds, ignite a passion for learning, and develop a deep-rooted understanding of mathematical concepts.

Picture this: your child eagerly delves into the pages of Mathflare Workbook, greeted by a step-by-step guide illuminated with vivid examples that demystify complex mathematical concepts. With each turn of the page, they embark on a journey of discovery, encountering thoughtfully curated practice questions that reinforce learning and hone problem-solving skills. And when they unveil the answers to those very questions, a sense of accomplishment blossoms within them – a tangible reward for their hard work and dedication.

But MathFlare Workbooks are more than just tools for learning; they are pathways to comprehension, fostering a deep-seated understanding of mathematical concepts through a sequential, logical flow. From fundamental principles to advanced problem-solving strategies, every chapter builds upon the last, ensuring a robust foundation upon which future knowledge can be constructed.

As parents, we yearn for nothing more than to see our children thrive, to witness the spark of inspiration ignited within them as they conquer academic challenges with confidence and poise. MathFlare Workbooks serve as partners in this noble endeavor, offering not just practice questions, but the keys to unlocking a world of opportunity.

And for teachers, MathFlare Workbooks stand as invaluable allies in the quest to cultivate mathematical proficiency in the classroom. With answers readily available, instructors can focus on guiding and nurturing their students, confident in the knowledge that MathFlare Workbooks provide a solid framework upon which to build.

In the pages of MathFlare Workbooks, we find not just the promise of academic excellence, but the seeds of a brighter tomorrow. So let us embrace the power of mathematics, let us champion the journey of learning, and let us pave the way for a generation of young minds poised to shape the world. With MathFlare Workbooks as our guide, the possibilities are infinite, and the future, bright.

Table of Contents

MathFlare
MATH WORKBOOK
Grade 2
Step by Step Guide and Essential Practice with Answers
Addition Subtraction
Multiplication
Place Value and Expanded Notations
Geometry
MathFlare Publishing

MathFlare
MATH WORKBOOK
Grade 2-3
Step by Step Guide and Essential Practice with Answers
Addition Subtraction
Multiplication and Division
Place Value and Expanded Notations
Geometry
MathFlare Publishing

MathFlare
MATH WORKBOOK
Grade 3
Step by Step Guide and Essential Practice with Answers
Multiplication and Division
Decimals
Place Value and Expanded Notations
Fractions and Geometry
MathFlare Publishing

MathFlare
MATH WORKBOOK
Grade 1
Step by Step Guide and Essential Practice with Answers
Counting and Numbers
Addition and Subtraction
Place Value and Expanded Notations
Understanding Time
MathFlare Publishing

MathFlare
MATH WORKBOOK
Grade 1-2
Step by Step Guide and Essential Practice with Answers
Counting and Numbers
Addition and Subtraction
Place Value and Expanded Notations
Understanding Time
MathFlare Publishing

MathFlare
MATH WORKBOOK
Grade 3-4
Step by Step Guide and Essential Practice with Answers
Addition Subtraction
Multiplication Division
Place Value and Expanded Notations
Fractions and Geometry
MathFlare Publishing

MathFlare
MATH WORKBOOK
Grade 4
Step by Step Guide and Essential Practice with Answers
Addition Subtraction
Multiplication Division
Place Value and Expanded Notations
Fractions and Geometry
MathFlare Publishing

MathFlare
MATH WORKBOOK
Grade 4-5
Step by Step Guide and Essential Practice with Answers
Multiplication Division
Place Value and Expanded Notations
Fractions and Geometry
Unit Conversion
MathFlare Publishing

MathFlare
Grade 5
MATH WORKBOOK
Step by Step Guide and Essential Practice with Answers
Multiplication Division
Place Value and Expanded Notations
Fractions and Geometry
Unit Conversion
MathFlare Publishing

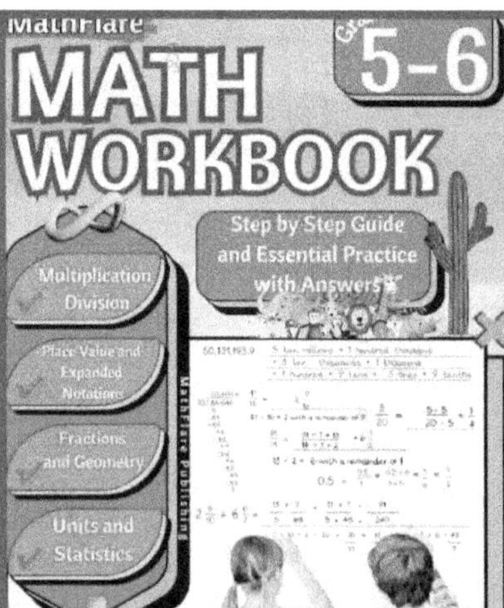
MathFlare
Grade 5-6
MATH WORKBOOK
Step by Step Guide and Essential Practice with Answers
Multiplication Division
Place Value and Expanded Notations
Fractions and Geometry
Units and Statistics
MathFlare Publishing

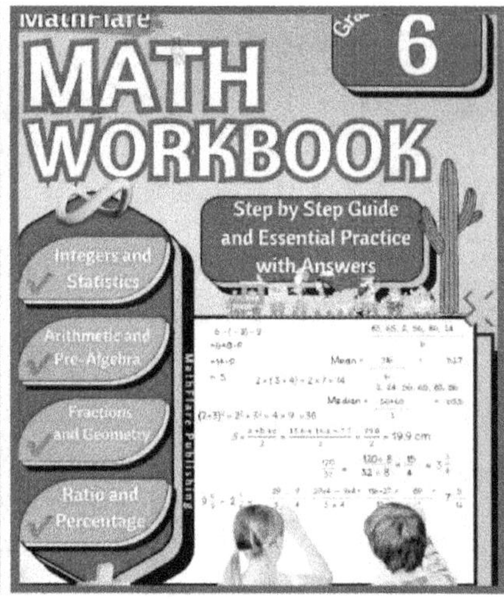
MathFlare
Grade 6
MATH WORKBOOK
Step by Step Guide and Essential Practice with Answers
Integers and Statistics
Arithmetic and Pre-Algebra
Fractions and Geometry
Ratio and Percentage
MathFlare Publishing

MathFlare
Grade 6-7
MATH WORKBOOK
Step by Step Guide and Essential Practice with Answers
Arithmetic and Pre-Algebra
Ratio, Percent Proportion
Geometry
Statistics
MathFlare Publishing

MathFlare
Grade 7
MATH WORKBOOK
Step by Step Guide and Essential Practice with Answers
Pre-Algebra
Ratio, Percent Proportion
Geometry
Statistics
MathFlare Publishing

MathFlare
Grade 7-8
MATH WORKBOOK
Step by Step Guide and Essential Practice with Answers
Pre-Algebra
Ratio, Percent Proportion
Geometry and Cartesian Plane
Statistics
MathFlare Publishing

MathFlare
Grade 8-9
MATH WORKBOOK
Step by Step Guide and Essential Practice with Answers
Pre-Algebra
Ratio, Proportion and Percentage
Linear Equations
Geometry and Cartesian Plane
MathFlare Publishing

MathFlare
Grade 8
MATH WORKBOOK
Step by Step Guide and Essential Practice with Answers
Pre-Algebra
Percentage
Linear Equations
Geometry
MathFlare Publishing

Fractions

Fractions represent parts of a whole. They consist of a numerator (the number on top) and a denominator (the number on the bottom).

For example: we have an orange, and we divide it into 5 equal slices. Each slice represents $\frac{1}{5}$ of the orange. Now, if we take 3 of those slices, we have taken $\frac{3}{5}$ of the orange.

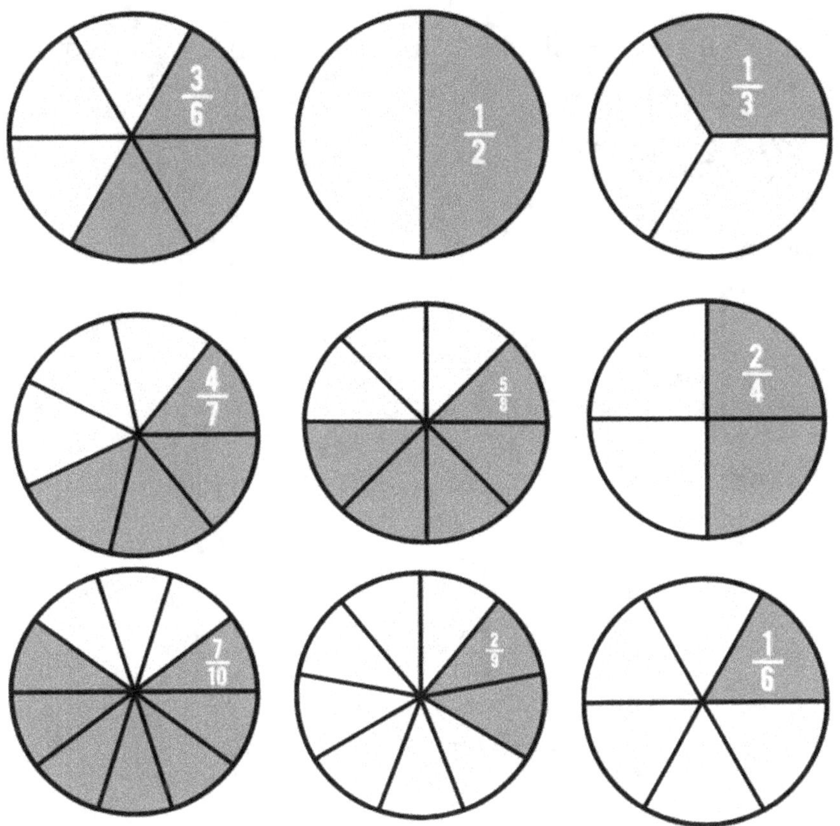

Equivalent Fractions

Equivalent fractions are fractions that represent the same value or part of a whole, even though they may look different.

To find equivalent fractions, you can:

- Multiply or divide both the numerator and denominator by the same nonzero number.
- Simplify fractions to their simplest form.

$\frac{1}{2}$ and $\frac{2}{4}$ are equivalent fractions because if you multiply the numerator and denominator of $\frac{1}{2}$ by 2, you get $\frac{2}{4}$. Similarly, if you divide both the numerator and denominator of $\frac{2}{4}$ by 2, you get $\frac{1}{2}$.

Let's solve a problem:

$$\frac{}{8} = \frac{15}{40}$$

To solve the missing numerator, we can cross multiply.

$$40x = 8 \times 15$$

$$40x = 120$$

$$x = \frac{120}{40} = x = 3$$

$$\frac{3}{8} = \frac{15}{40}$$

Fractions Addition (Common Denominator)

To add fractions with a common denominator, we add their numerators together and keep the denominator the same.

For example: if we want to add $\dfrac{3}{5}$ and $\dfrac{2}{5}$ both fractions have the same denominator of 5.

Therefore, to add them, we simply add their numerators:

$$\frac{3}{5} + \frac{2}{5} = \frac{3+2}{5} = \frac{5}{5}$$

Let's solve a problem:

$$\frac{9}{17} + \frac{1}{17} = \frac{9+1}{17} = \frac{10}{17}$$

Fractions Subtraction (Common Denominator)

To subtract fractions with a common denominator, we find the difference between their numerators and keep the denominator the same.

For example:

$$\frac{3}{5} - \frac{2}{5} = \frac{3-2}{5} = \frac{1}{5}$$

Let's solve a problem:

$$\frac{15}{16} - \frac{12}{16} = \frac{15-12}{16} = \frac{3}{16}$$

Fractions Multiplication

To multiply fractions, we simply multiply the numerators together to get the new numerator and multiply the denominators together to get the new denominator.

For example, let's multiply: $\dfrac{2}{4} \times \dfrac{1}{4}$

Numerator: 2 × 1 = 2

Denominator: 4 × 4 = 16

Therefore, $\dfrac{2}{16}$

we can simplify the resulting fraction:

$$\dfrac{1}{8}$$

Let's solve a problem:

$$\dfrac{4}{5} \times \dfrac{4}{5} = \dfrac{4 \times 4}{5 \times 5} = \dfrac{16}{25}$$

Fractions Division

To divide fractions, we multiply by the reciprocal of the divisor.

For example, let's divide:

$$\dfrac{6}{8} \div \dfrac{4}{8}$$

$$\dfrac{6}{8} \times \dfrac{8}{4} = \dfrac{48}{32} = \dfrac{3}{2}$$

Fraction Identification

Identify fractions of each set of boxes.

1. _______________ =

2. _______________ =

3. _______________ =

4. _______________ =

5. _______________ =

6. _______________ =

7. _______________ =

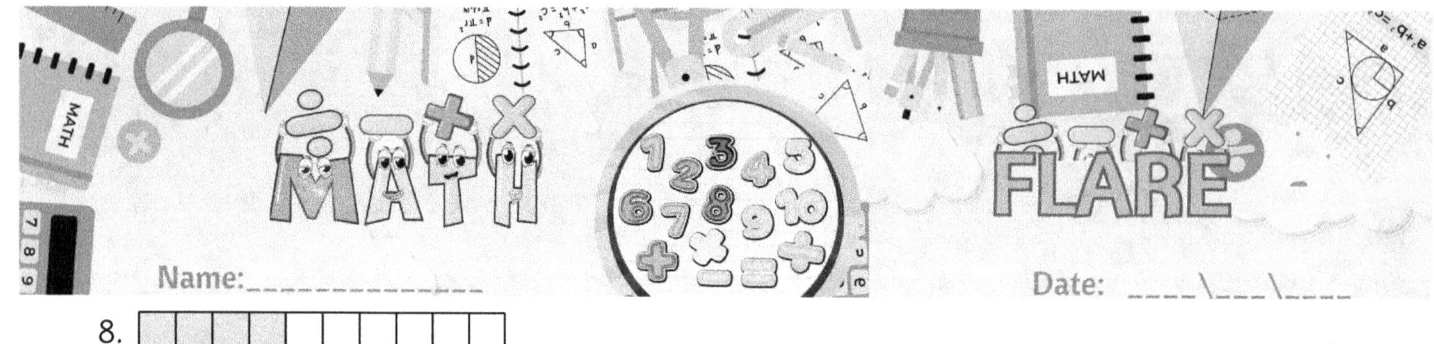

8.  = ________________

9. [ ] = ________________

10. [ ] = ________________

11. [ ] = ________________

12. [ ] = ________________

13. [ ] = ________________

14. [ ] = ________________

15. [ ] = ________________

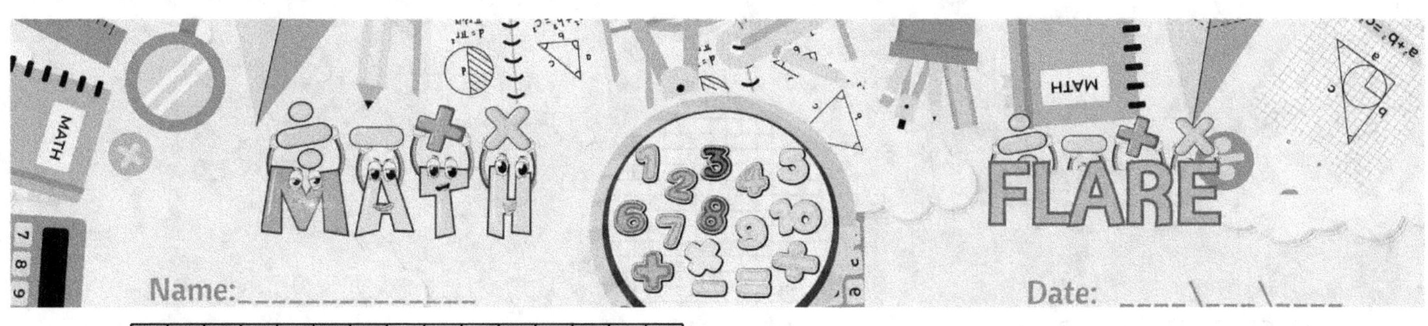

16. 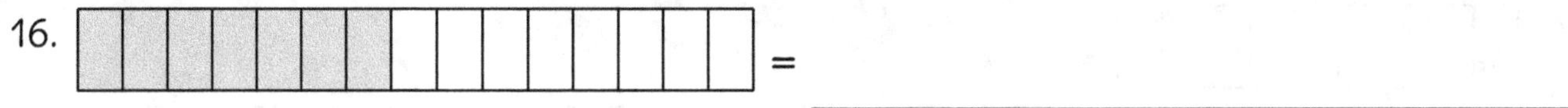 = ______________________________

17. = ______________________________

18. = ______________________________

19. = ______________________________

20. = ______________________________

21. = ______________________________

22. = ______________________________

23. = ______________________________

24. 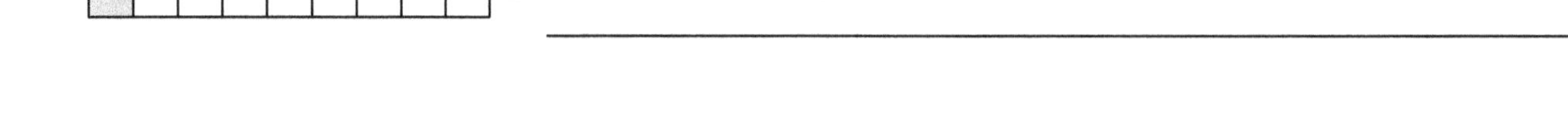 = ____________________________

25. = ____________________________

26. = ____________________________

27. = ____________________________

28. 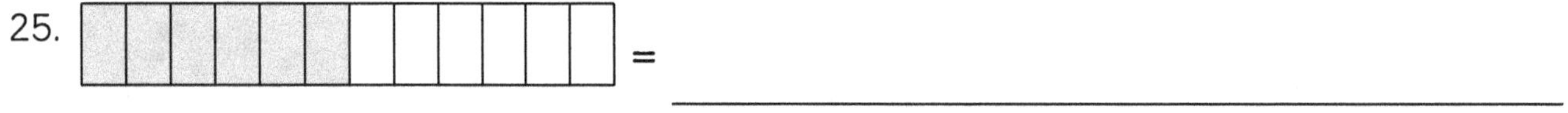 = ____________________________

29. = ____________________________

30. = ____________________________

31. = ____________________________

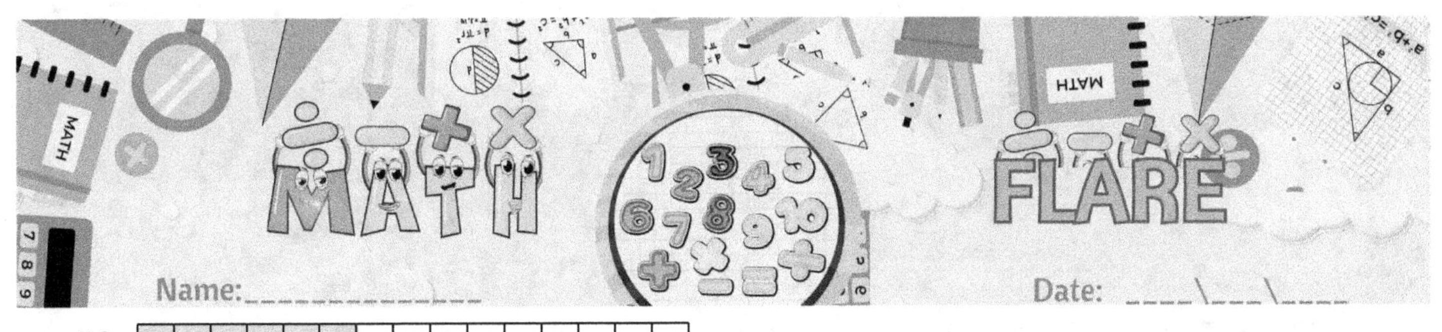

Name:____________________   Date: _______________

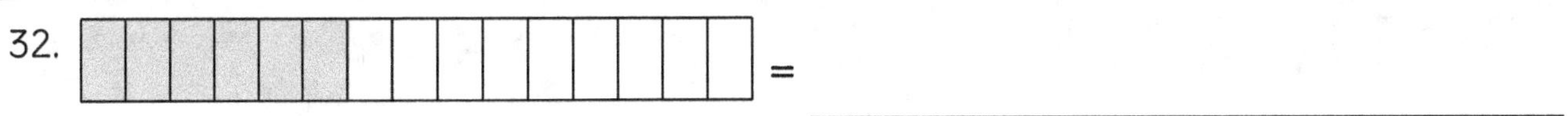

32. = ________________________

33. = ________________________

34. = ________________________

35. = ________________________

36. = ________________________

37. = ________________________

38. = ________________________

39. = ________________________

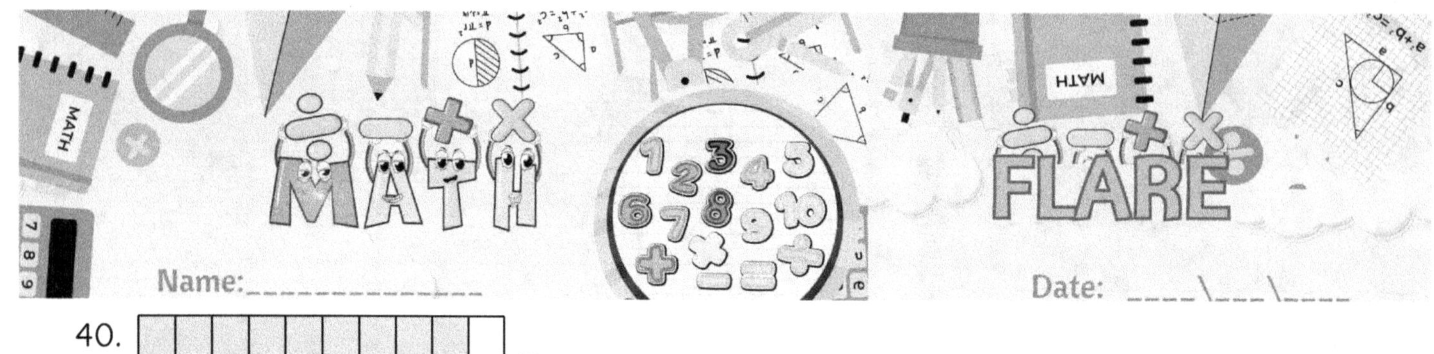

40. 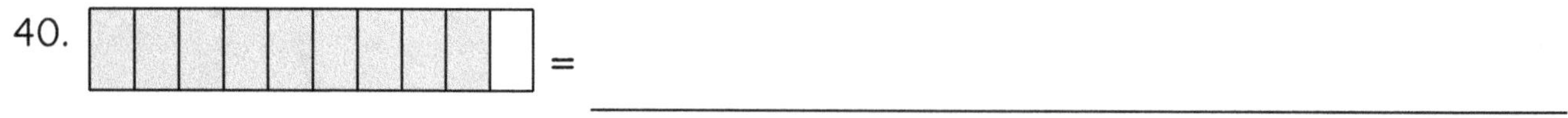 = _______________________

41. 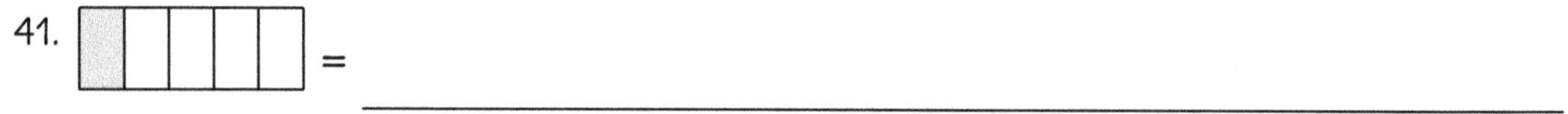 = _______________________

42. = _______________________

43. = _______________________

44. = _______________________

45. = _______________________

46. = _______________________

47. = _______________________

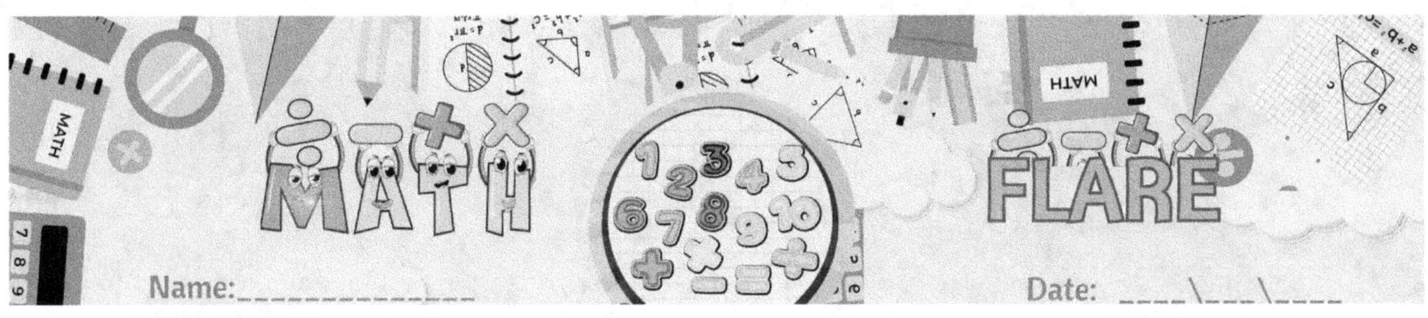

48. = _______________________________

49. = _______________________________

50. = _______________________________

51. = _______________________________

52. = _______________________________

53. = _______________________________

54. = _______________________________

55. = _______________________________

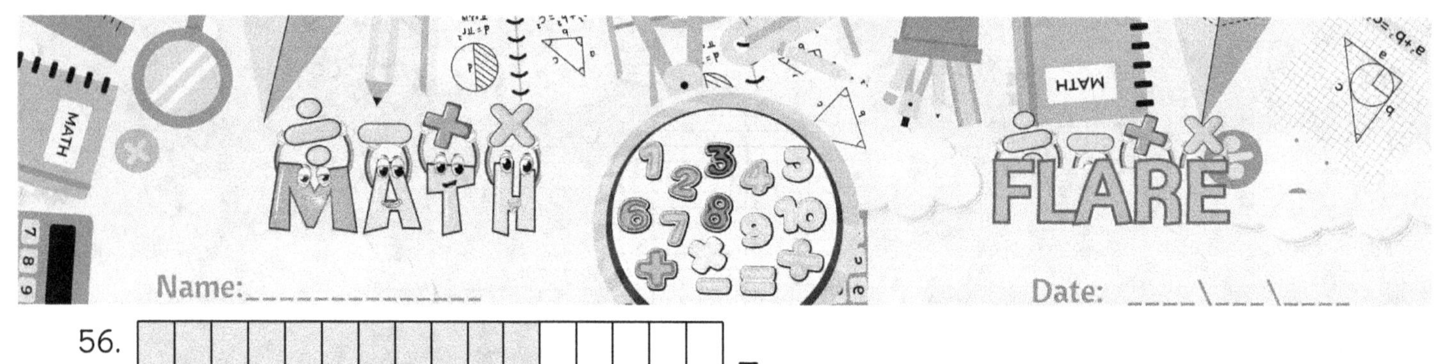

56. 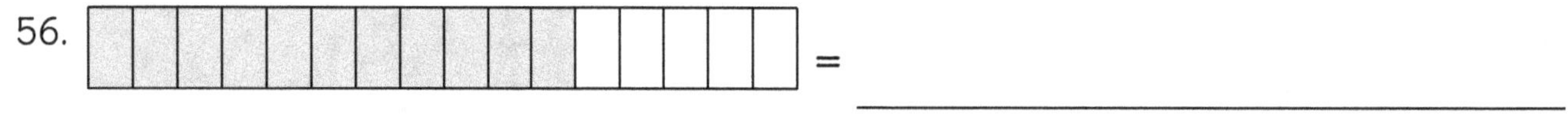 = ________________________

57. 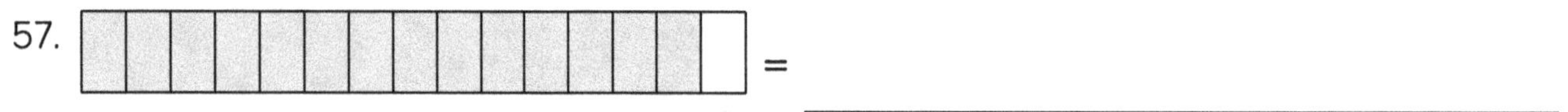 = ________________________

58. = ________________________

59. 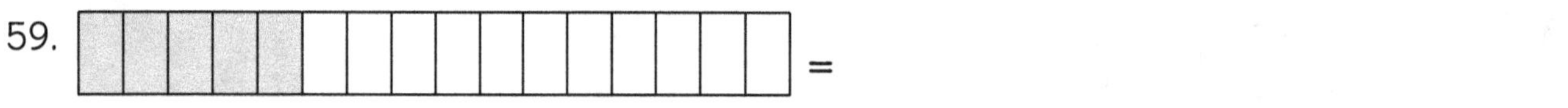 = ________________________

60.  = ________________________

61. = ________________________

62. = ________________________

63. = ________________________

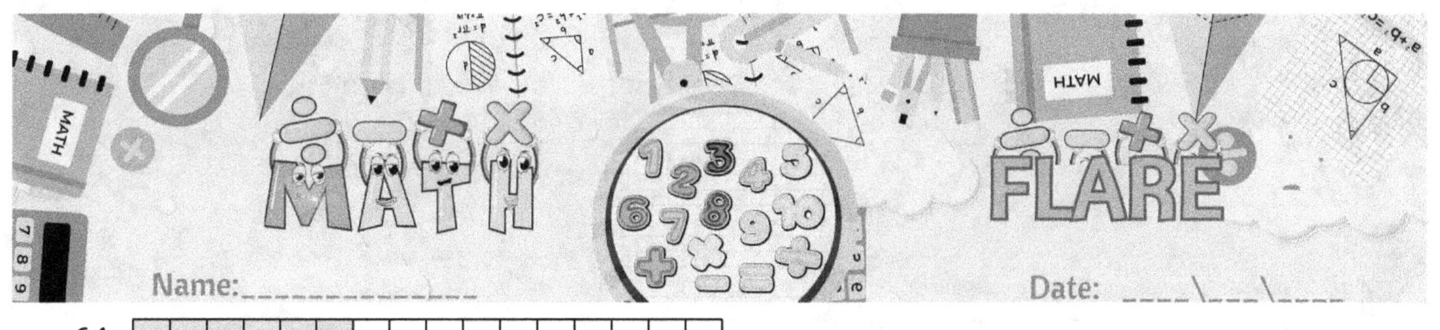

64. 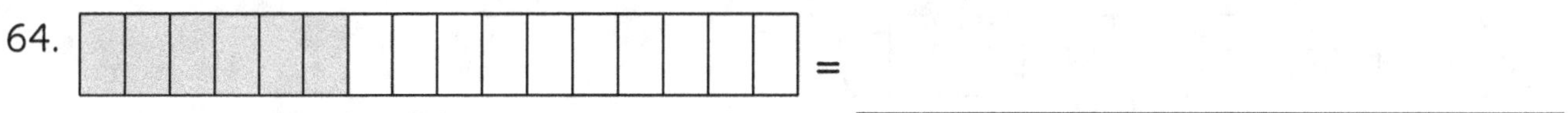 = _______________________

65. = _______________________

66. = _______________________

67. = _______________________

68. = _______________________

69. = _______________________

70. = _______________________

71. = _______________________

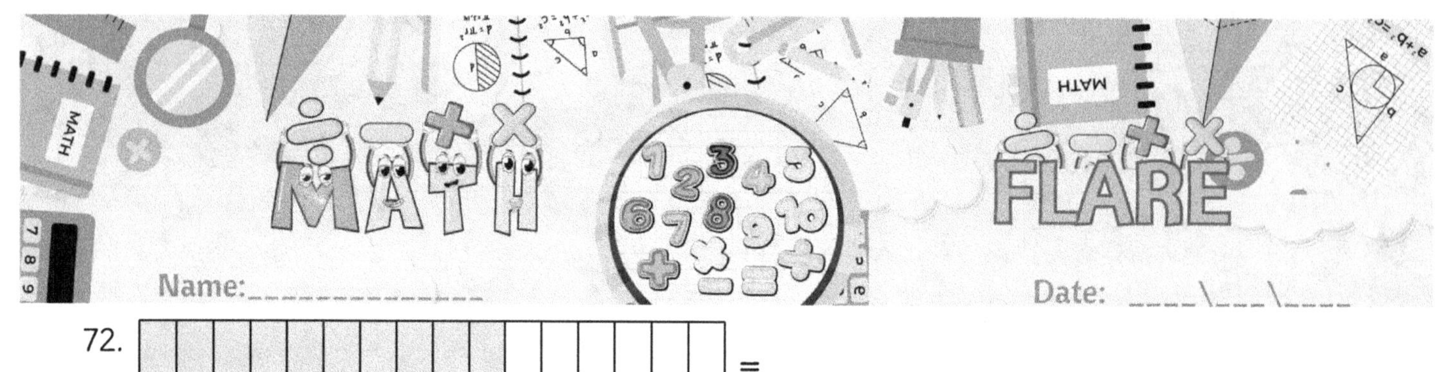

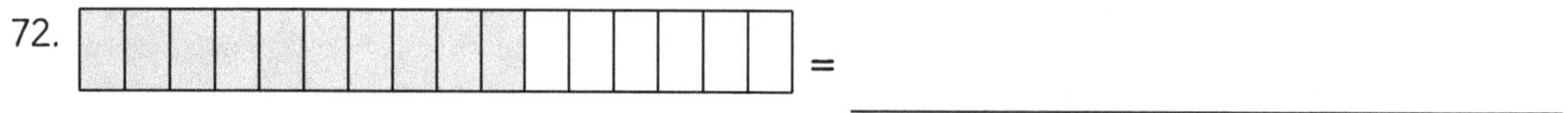

72. = ________________________

73. = ________________________

74. = ________________________

75. = ________________________

76. = ________________________

77. = ________________________

78. = ________________________

79. = ________________________

Compare the Fractions

Compare the fractions. Put the signs < , >, or =

1. $\dfrac{17}{8}$ ___ $\dfrac{2}{8}$

2. $\dfrac{2}{3}$ ___ $\dfrac{2}{3}$

3. $\dfrac{36}{13}$ ___ $\dfrac{5}{13}$

4. $\dfrac{18}{17}$ ___ $\dfrac{16}{17}$

5. $\dfrac{10}{22}$ ___ $\dfrac{39}{22}$

6. $\dfrac{90}{144}$ ___ $\dfrac{72}{144}$

7. $\dfrac{20}{9}$ ___ $\dfrac{2}{9}$

8. $\dfrac{4}{18}$ ___ $\dfrac{17}{18}$

9. $\dfrac{5}{10}$ ___ $\dfrac{8}{10}$

10. $\dfrac{72}{76}$ ___ $\dfrac{41}{76}$

11. $\dfrac{5}{10}$ ___ $\dfrac{9}{10}$

12. $\dfrac{4}{14}$ ___ $\dfrac{1}{14}$

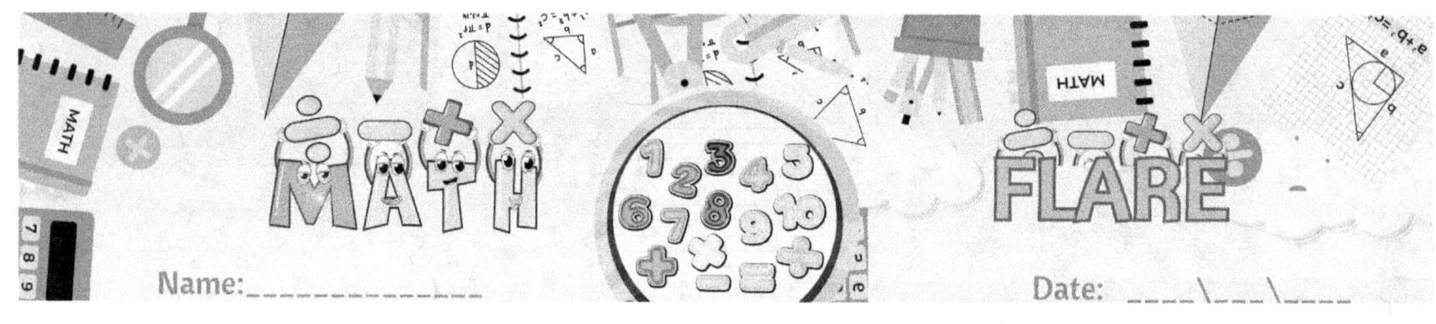

13. $\dfrac{3}{7}$ ___ $\dfrac{4}{7}$

14. $\dfrac{6}{8}$ ___ $\dfrac{5}{8}$

15. $\dfrac{4}{12}$ ___ $\dfrac{4}{12}$

16. $\dfrac{4}{5}$ ___ $\dfrac{1}{5}$

17. $\dfrac{30}{11}$ ___ $\dfrac{21}{11}$

18. $\dfrac{18}{21}$ ___ $\dfrac{34}{21}$

19. $\dfrac{72}{80}$ ___ $\dfrac{19}{80}$

20. $\dfrac{10}{6}$ ___ $\dfrac{4}{6}$

21. $\dfrac{10}{7}$ ___ $\dfrac{3}{7}$

22. $\dfrac{36}{96}$ ___ $\dfrac{14}{96}$

23. $\dfrac{12}{48}$ ___ $\dfrac{31}{48}$

24. $\dfrac{12}{60}$ ___ $\dfrac{117}{60}$

25. $\dfrac{1}{6}$ ___ $\dfrac{4}{6}$

26. $\dfrac{3}{2}$ ___ $\dfrac{1}{2}$

27. $\dfrac{7}{9}$ ___ $\dfrac{6}{9}$

28. $\dfrac{12}{52}$ ___ $\dfrac{10}{52}$

29. $\dfrac{49}{19}$ ___ $\dfrac{2}{19}$

30. $\dfrac{11}{12}$ ___ $\dfrac{2}{12}$

31. $\dfrac{14}{20}$ ___ $\dfrac{43}{20}$

32. $\dfrac{35}{70}$ ___ $\dfrac{44}{70}$

33. $\dfrac{49}{22}$ ___ $\dfrac{12}{22}$

34. $\dfrac{1}{3}$ ___ $\dfrac{1}{3}$

35. $\dfrac{24}{11}$ ___ $\dfrac{1}{11}$

36. $\dfrac{51}{24}$ ___ $\dfrac{25}{24}$

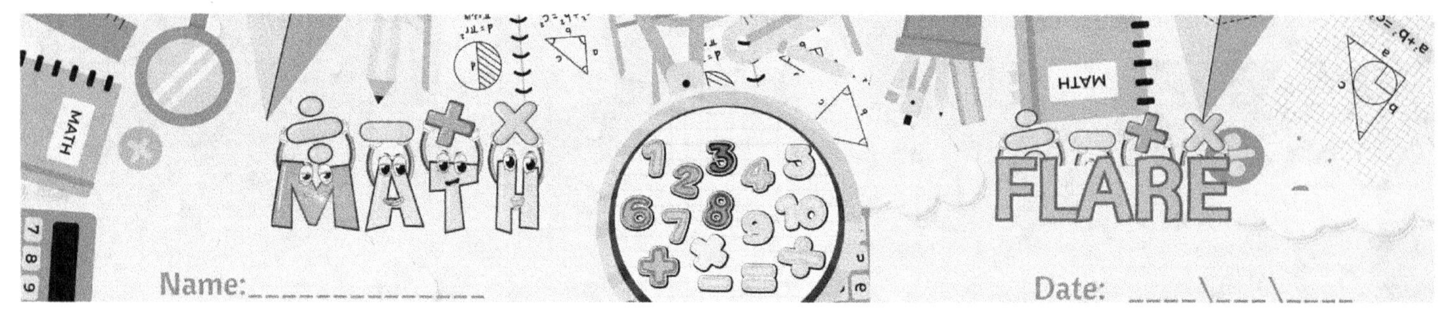

37. $\dfrac{38}{21}$ ___ $\dfrac{38}{21}$

38. $\dfrac{2}{4}$ ___ $\dfrac{1}{4}$

39. $\dfrac{48}{17}$ ___ $\dfrac{10}{17}$

40. $\dfrac{73}{25}$ ___ $\dfrac{22}{25}$

41. $\dfrac{66}{90}$ ___ $\dfrac{107}{90}$

42. $\dfrac{4}{20}$ ___ $\dfrac{29}{20}$

43. $\dfrac{29}{23}$ ___ $\dfrac{21}{23}$

44. $\dfrac{55}{30}$ ___ $\dfrac{89}{30}$

45. $\dfrac{48}{18}$ ___ $\dfrac{2}{18}$

46. $\dfrac{20}{48}$ ___ $\dfrac{27}{48}$

47. $\dfrac{8}{6}$ ___ $\dfrac{9}{6}$

48. $\dfrac{40}{100}$ ___ $\dfrac{64}{100}$

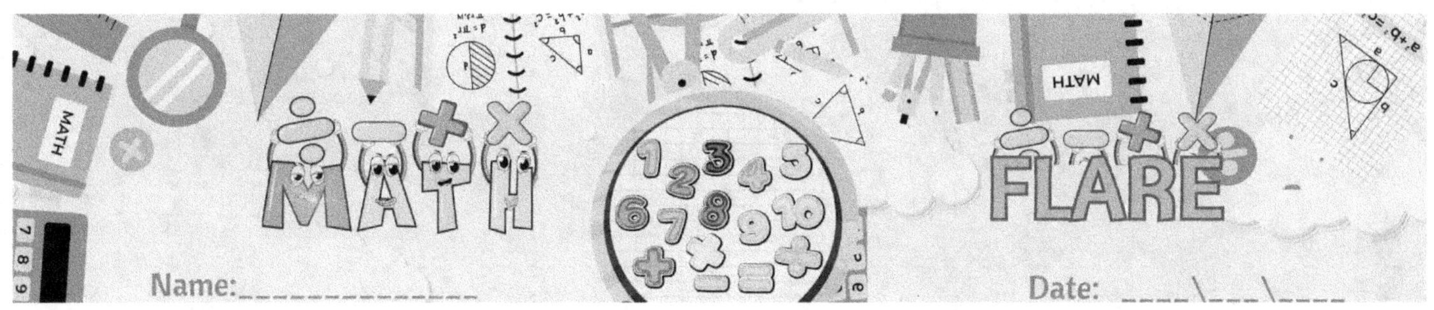

49. $\dfrac{9}{13}$ ___ $\dfrac{15}{13}$

50. $\dfrac{52}{23}$ ___ $\dfrac{15}{23}$

51. $\dfrac{20}{40}$ ___ $\dfrac{39}{40}$

52. $\dfrac{13}{21}$ ___ $\dfrac{59}{21}$

53. $\dfrac{1}{3}$ ___ $\dfrac{2}{3}$

54. $\dfrac{3}{12}$ ___ $\dfrac{31}{12}$

55. $\dfrac{12}{57}$ ___ $\dfrac{15}{57}$

56. $\dfrac{20}{110}$ ___ $\dfrac{52}{110}$

57. $\dfrac{37}{24}$ ___ $\dfrac{56}{24}$

58. $\dfrac{25}{40}$ ___ $\dfrac{33}{40}$

59. $\dfrac{45}{55}$ ___ $\dfrac{44}{55}$

60. $\dfrac{36}{50}$ ___ $\dfrac{120}{50}$

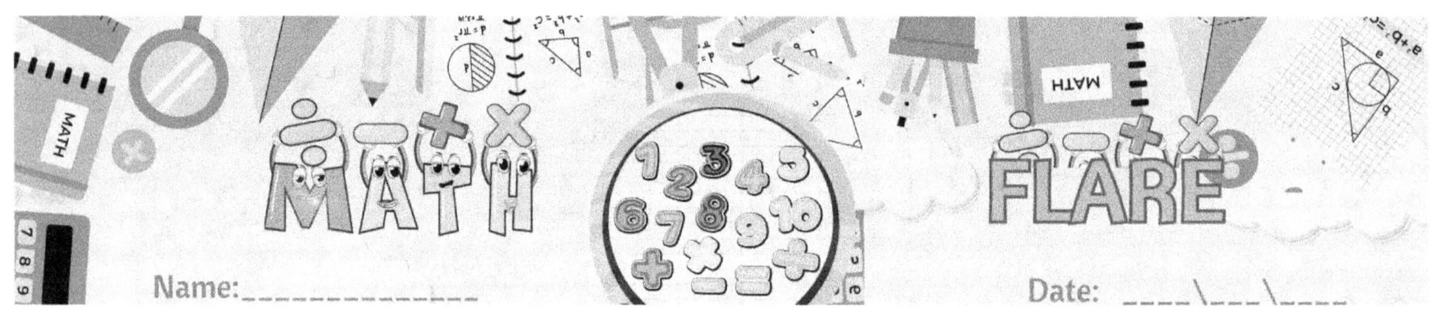

61. $\dfrac{35}{18}$ ___ $\dfrac{9}{18}$

62. $\dfrac{5}{2}$ ___ $\dfrac{3}{2}$

63. $\dfrac{15}{21}$ ___ $\dfrac{40}{21}$

64. $\dfrac{24}{30}$ ___ $\dfrac{9}{30}$

65. $\dfrac{12}{56}$ ___ $\dfrac{133}{56}$

66. $\dfrac{32}{68}$ ___ $\dfrac{47}{68}$

67. $\dfrac{15}{27}$ ___ $\dfrac{25}{27}$

68. $\dfrac{45}{48}$ ___ $\dfrac{37}{48}$

69. $\dfrac{89}{30}$ ___ $\dfrac{72}{30}$

70. $\dfrac{14}{15}$ ___ $\dfrac{14}{15}$

71. $\dfrac{12}{14}$ ___ $\dfrac{1}{14}$

72. $\dfrac{54}{72}$ ___ $\dfrac{75}{72}$

73. $\dfrac{5}{15}$ ___ $\dfrac{33}{15}$

74. $\dfrac{4}{3}$ ___ $\dfrac{1}{3}$

75. $\dfrac{36}{54}$ ___ $\dfrac{30}{54}$

76. $\dfrac{3}{6}$ ___ $\dfrac{3}{6}$

77. $\dfrac{14}{6}$ ___ $\dfrac{5}{6}$

78. $\dfrac{1}{18}$ ___ $\dfrac{8}{18}$

79. $\dfrac{3}{19}$ ___ $\dfrac{29}{19}$

80. $\dfrac{57}{23}$ ___ $\dfrac{6}{23}$

81. $\dfrac{23}{24}$ ___ $\dfrac{22}{24}$

82. $\dfrac{2}{26}$ ___ $\dfrac{25}{26}$

83. $\dfrac{6}{75}$ ___ $\dfrac{35}{75}$

84. $\dfrac{30}{20}$ ___ $\dfrac{22}{20}$

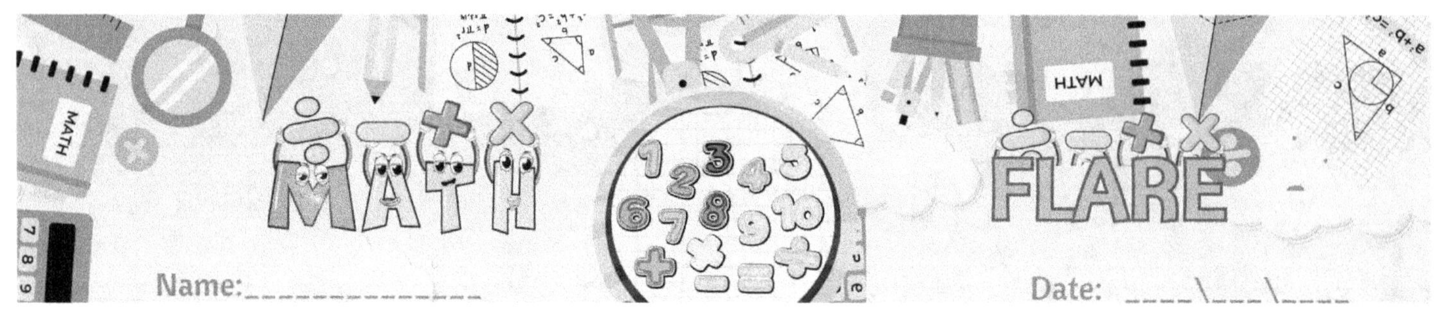

85. $\dfrac{48}{132}$ ___ $\dfrac{64}{132}$

86. $\dfrac{19}{21}$ ___ $\dfrac{33}{21}$

87. $\dfrac{9}{21}$ ___ $\dfrac{8}{21}$

88. $\dfrac{6}{11}$ ___ $\dfrac{10}{11}$

89. $\dfrac{5}{8}$ ___ $\dfrac{2}{8}$

90. $\dfrac{2}{10}$ ___ $\dfrac{8}{10}$

91. $\dfrac{17}{30}$ ___ $\dfrac{18}{30}$

92. $\dfrac{2}{5}$ ___ $\dfrac{14}{5}$

93. $\dfrac{44}{16}$ ___ $\dfrac{12}{16}$

94. $\dfrac{1}{4}$ ___ $\dfrac{6}{4}$

95. $\dfrac{45}{17}$ ___ $\dfrac{5}{17}$

96. $\dfrac{5}{35}$ ___ $\dfrac{4}{35}$

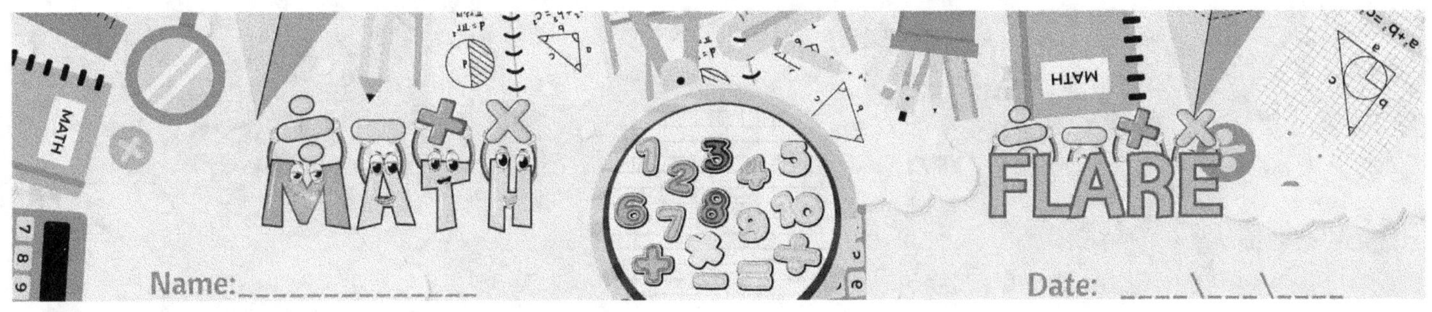

Equivalent Fractions

1. $\dfrac{1}{} = \dfrac{4}{28}$

2. $\dfrac{5}{} = \dfrac{40}{72}$

3. $\dfrac{}{19} = \dfrac{16}{38}$

4. $\dfrac{1}{10} = \dfrac{}{60}$

5. $\dfrac{}{18} = \dfrac{136}{144}$

6. $\dfrac{3}{14} = \dfrac{21}{}$

7. $\dfrac{7}{8} = \dfrac{70}{}$

8. $\dfrac{2}{3} = \dfrac{18}{}$

9. $\dfrac{1}{5} = \dfrac{}{20}$

10. $\dfrac{7}{} = \dfrac{35}{100}$

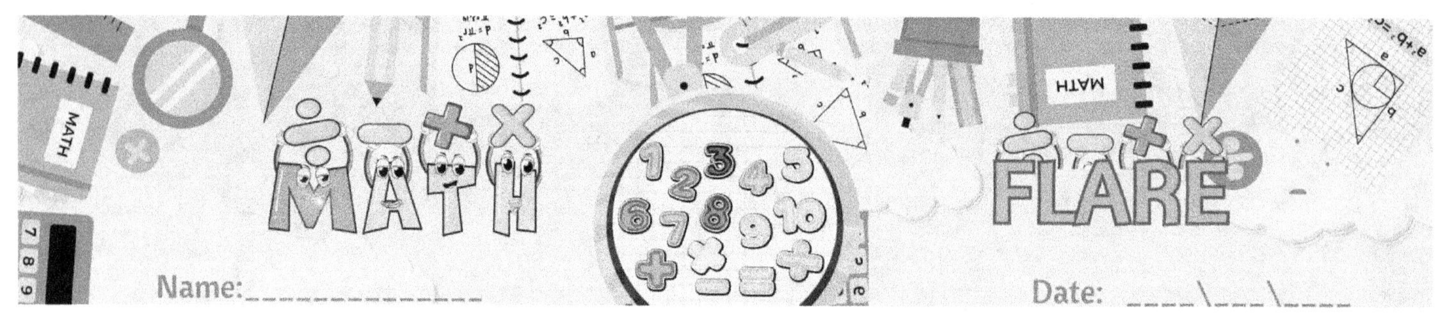

11. $\dfrac{}{17} = \dfrac{90}{102}$

12. $\dfrac{7}{} = \dfrac{63}{135}$

13. $\dfrac{12}{13} = \dfrac{}{78}$

14. $\dfrac{}{12} = \dfrac{16}{48}$

15. $\dfrac{3}{} = \dfrac{6}{8}$

16. $\dfrac{5}{7} = \dfrac{10}{}$

17. $\dfrac{3}{} = \dfrac{12}{64}$

18. $\dfrac{}{11} = \dfrac{14}{22}$

19. $\dfrac{5}{6} = \dfrac{}{48}$

20. $\dfrac{1}{} = \dfrac{7}{14}$

21. $\dfrac{9}{16} = \dfrac{45}{}$

22. $\dfrac{1}{14} = \dfrac{8}{}$

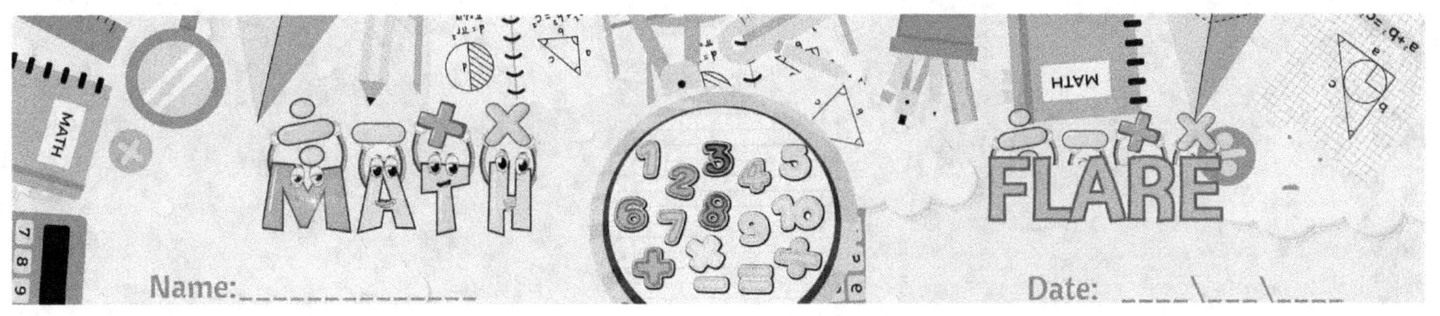

23. $\dfrac{5}{11} = \dfrac{}{110}$

24. $\dfrac{6}{} = \dfrac{12}{26}$

25. $\dfrac{1}{2} = \dfrac{}{18}$

26. $\dfrac{3}{} = \dfrac{15}{35}$

27. $\dfrac{11}{19} = \dfrac{}{76}$

28. $\dfrac{7}{18} = \dfrac{}{36}$

29. $\dfrac{10}{15} = \dfrac{}{90}$

30. $\dfrac{3}{4} = \dfrac{}{28}$

31. $\dfrac{18}{20} = \dfrac{180}{}$

32. $\dfrac{}{10} = \dfrac{4}{20}$

33. $\dfrac{8}{12} = \dfrac{}{24}$

34. $\dfrac{2}{3} = \dfrac{16}{}$

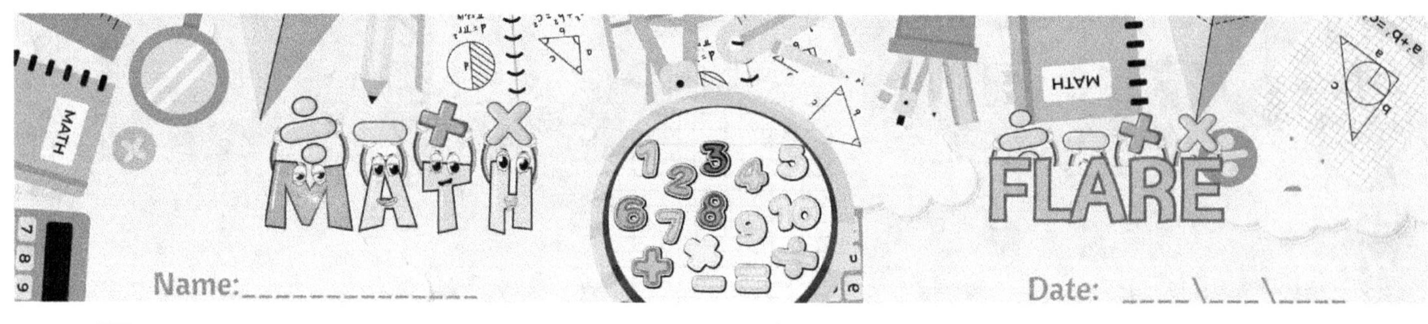

35. $\dfrac{3}{5} = \dfrac{18}{}$

36. $\dfrac{13}{} = \dfrac{65}{85}$

37. $\dfrac{}{9} = \dfrac{60}{90}$

38. $\dfrac{6}{8} = \dfrac{24}{}$

39. $\dfrac{}{6} = \dfrac{8}{12}$

40. $\dfrac{8}{19} = \dfrac{48}{}$

41. $\dfrac{5}{13} = \dfrac{}{39}$

42. $\dfrac{8}{9} = \dfrac{80}{}$

43. $\dfrac{}{12} = \dfrac{88}{96}$

44. $\dfrac{1}{2} = \dfrac{}{12}$

45. $\dfrac{}{3} = \dfrac{3}{9}$

46. $\dfrac{1}{4} = \dfrac{}{8}$

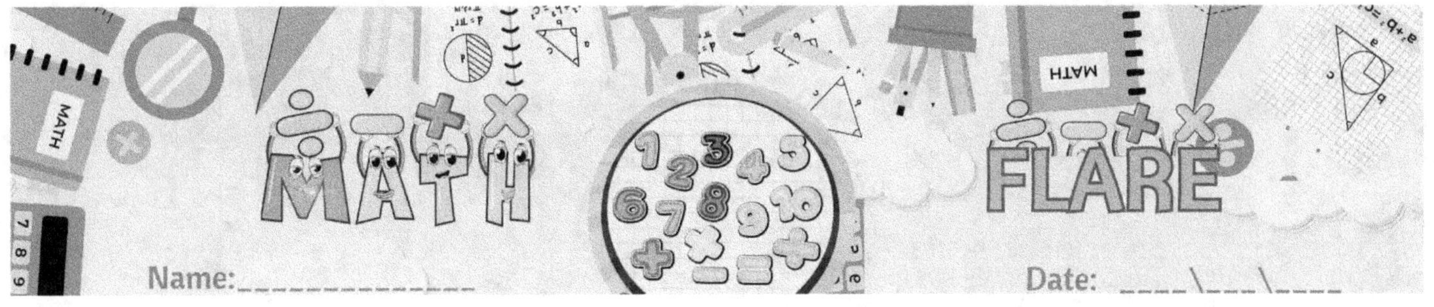

47. $\dfrac{1}{8} = \dfrac{2}{}$

48. $\dfrac{1}{17} = \dfrac{3}{}$

49. $\dfrac{6}{19} = \dfrac{}{114}$

50. $\dfrac{}{12} = \dfrac{20}{24}$

51. $\dfrac{2}{4} = \dfrac{16}{}$

52. $\dfrac{8}{} = \dfrac{16}{28}$

53. $\dfrac{3}{} = \dfrac{18}{54}$

54. $\dfrac{7}{} = \dfrac{21}{33}$

55. $\dfrac{}{15} = \dfrac{64}{120}$

56. $\dfrac{1}{5} = \dfrac{}{45}$

57. $\dfrac{17}{} = \dfrac{170}{180}$

58. $\dfrac{6}{} = \dfrac{48}{56}$

59. $\dfrac{11}{20} = \dfrac{}{100}$

60. $\dfrac{10}{17} = \dfrac{}{85}$

61. $\dfrac{6}{10} = \dfrac{60}{}$

62. $\dfrac{2}{6} = \dfrac{8}{}$

63. $\dfrac{6}{16} = \dfrac{42}{}$

64. $\dfrac{}{3} = \dfrac{6}{18}$

65. $\dfrac{}{8} = \dfrac{30}{48}$

66. $\dfrac{10}{} = \dfrac{80}{104}$

67. $\dfrac{1}{} = \dfrac{9}{81}$

68. $\dfrac{}{6} = \dfrac{36}{54}$

69. $\dfrac{1}{} = \dfrac{8}{56}$

70. $\dfrac{2}{} = \dfrac{4}{30}$

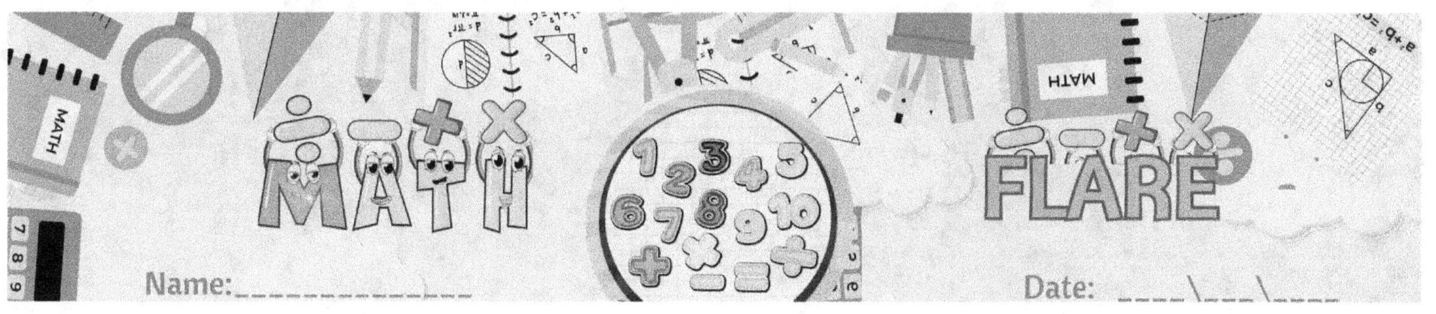

71. $\dfrac{3}{8} = \dfrac{}{16}$

72. $\dfrac{1}{10} = \dfrac{10}{}$

73. $\dfrac{2}{} = \dfrac{8}{20}$

74. $\dfrac{13}{17} = \dfrac{78}{}$

75. $\dfrac{2}{19} = \dfrac{}{190}$

76. $\dfrac{1}{20} = \dfrac{}{100}$

77. $\dfrac{2}{} = \dfrac{18}{36}$

78. $\dfrac{5}{18} = \dfrac{20}{}$

79. $\dfrac{7}{} = \dfrac{21}{39}$

80. $\dfrac{}{12} = \dfrac{14}{84}$

81. $\dfrac{}{11} = \dfrac{48}{66}$

82. $\dfrac{}{16} = \dfrac{18}{144}$

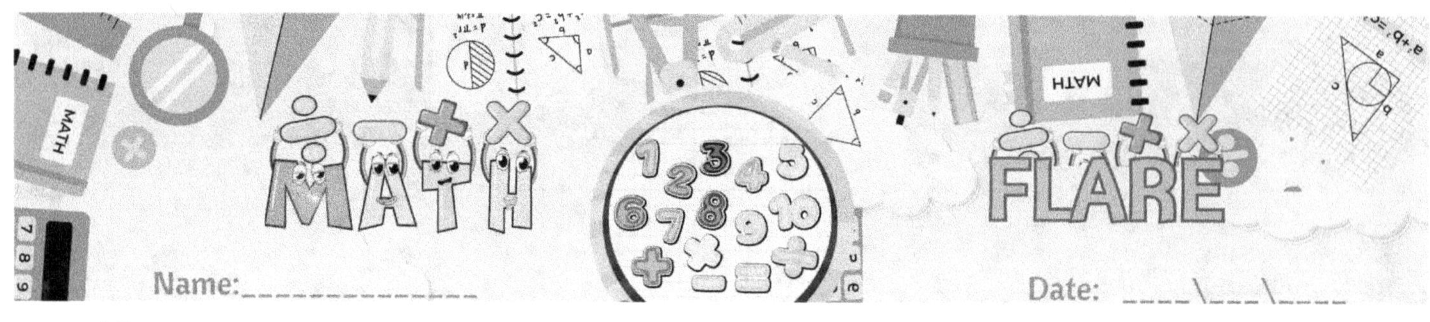

83. $\dfrac{5}{} = \dfrac{50}{140}$

84. $\dfrac{13}{} = \dfrac{78}{90}$

85. $\dfrac{2}{13} = \dfrac{20}{}$

86. $\dfrac{}{6} = \dfrac{20}{60}$

87. $\dfrac{}{7} = \dfrac{27}{63}$

88. $\dfrac{2}{3} = \dfrac{12}{}$

89. $\dfrac{6}{8} = \dfrac{60}{}$

90. $\dfrac{}{14} = \dfrac{78}{84}$

91. $\dfrac{}{10} = \dfrac{8}{80}$

92. $\dfrac{9}{} = \dfrac{27}{36}$

93. $\dfrac{15}{} = \dfrac{60}{76}$

94. $\dfrac{}{17} = \dfrac{70}{119}$

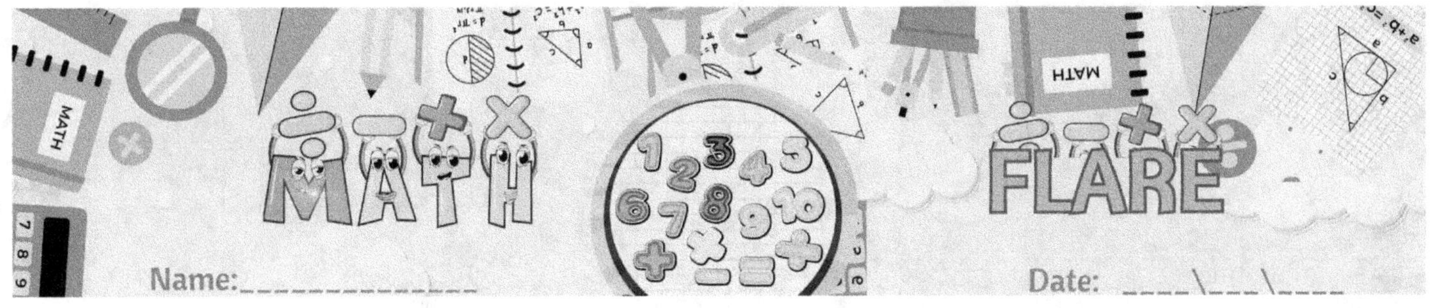

95. $\dfrac{2}{4} = \dfrac{}{8}$

96. $\dfrac{8}{} = \dfrac{16}{18}$

97. $\dfrac{2}{5} = \dfrac{16}{}$

98. $\dfrac{}{18} = \dfrac{45}{90}$

99. $\dfrac{1}{11} = \dfrac{4}{}$

100. $\dfrac{4}{16} = \dfrac{}{64}$

101. $\dfrac{3}{} = \dfrac{27}{180}$

102. $\dfrac{1}{} = \dfrac{10}{20}$

103. $\dfrac{4}{} = \dfrac{32}{136}$

104. $\dfrac{}{7} = \dfrac{8}{14}$

Fractions Addition: Common Denominator

Find the sum.

1. $\dfrac{1}{9} + \dfrac{5}{9} =$ _______________

2. $\dfrac{1}{6} + \dfrac{3}{6} =$ _______________

3. $\dfrac{6}{12} + \dfrac{3}{12} =$ _______________

4. $\dfrac{2}{5} + \dfrac{2}{5} =$ _______________

5. $\dfrac{1}{4} + \dfrac{2}{4} =$ _______________

6. $\dfrac{5}{11} + \dfrac{1}{11} =$ _______________

7. $\dfrac{1}{3} + \dfrac{1}{3} =$ _______________

8. $\dfrac{2}{8} + \dfrac{3}{8} =$ _______________

9. $\dfrac{1}{7} + \dfrac{2}{7} =$ _______________

10. $\dfrac{4}{10} + \dfrac{5}{10} =$ _______________

11. $\dfrac{6}{11} + \dfrac{2}{11} =$ _______________

12. $\dfrac{1}{12} + \dfrac{9}{12} =$ _______________

13. $\dfrac{5}{9} + \dfrac{2}{9} =$ _________________

14. $\dfrac{1}{2} + \dfrac{1}{2} =$ _________________

15. $\dfrac{3}{5} + \dfrac{1}{5} =$ _________________

16. $\dfrac{1}{6} + \dfrac{2}{6} =$ _________________

17. $\dfrac{4}{6} + \dfrac{1}{6} =$ _________________

18. $\dfrac{1}{5} + \dfrac{1}{5} =$ _________________

19. $\dfrac{10}{12} + \dfrac{1}{12} =$ _________________

20. $\dfrac{2}{7} + \dfrac{2}{7} =$ _________________

21. $\dfrac{3}{10} + \dfrac{5}{10} =$ _________________

22. $\dfrac{6}{11} + \dfrac{4}{11} =$ _________________

23. $\dfrac{1}{4} + \dfrac{1}{4} =$ _________________

24. $\dfrac{2}{7} + \dfrac{3}{7} =$ _________________

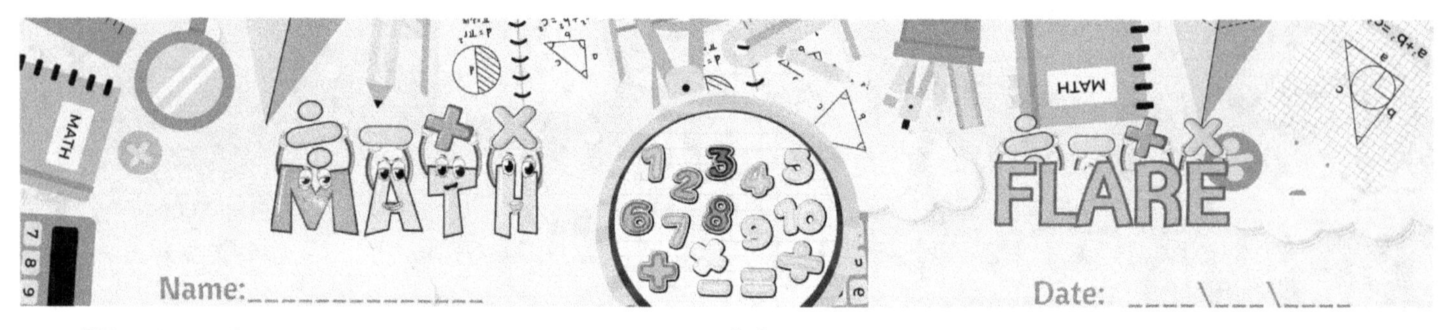

25. $\dfrac{4}{8} + \dfrac{2}{8} =$ _________________

26. $\dfrac{3}{12} + \dfrac{2}{12} =$ _________________

27. $\dfrac{1}{11} + \dfrac{8}{11} =$ _________________

28. $\dfrac{2}{9} + \dfrac{5}{9} =$ _________________

29. $\dfrac{2}{5} + \dfrac{1}{5} =$ _________________

30. $\dfrac{4}{10} + \dfrac{4}{10} =$ _________________

31. $\dfrac{5}{11} + \dfrac{4}{11} =$ _________________

32. $\dfrac{2}{10} + \dfrac{3}{10} =$ _________________

33. $\dfrac{2}{12} + \dfrac{4}{12} =$ _________________

34. $\dfrac{3}{8} + \dfrac{3}{8} =$ _________________

35. $\dfrac{3}{7} + \dfrac{3}{7} =$ _________________

36. $\dfrac{1}{6} + \dfrac{4}{6} =$ _________________

37. $\dfrac{5}{9} + \dfrac{1}{9} =$ _______________

38. $\dfrac{3}{7} + \dfrac{2}{7} =$ _______________

39. $\dfrac{4}{10} + \dfrac{2}{10} =$ _______________

40. $\dfrac{2}{8} + \dfrac{1}{8} =$ _______________

41. $\dfrac{4}{11} + \dfrac{1}{11} =$ _______________

42. $\dfrac{5}{12} + \dfrac{5}{12} =$ _______________

43. $\dfrac{1}{5} + \dfrac{3}{5} =$ _______________

44. $\dfrac{5}{12} + \dfrac{3}{12} =$ _______________

45. $\dfrac{4}{9} + \dfrac{3}{9} =$ _______________

46. $\dfrac{2}{6} + \dfrac{2}{6} =$ _______________

47. $\dfrac{6}{10} + \dfrac{1}{10} =$ _______________

48. $\dfrac{2}{11} + \dfrac{4}{11} =$ _______________

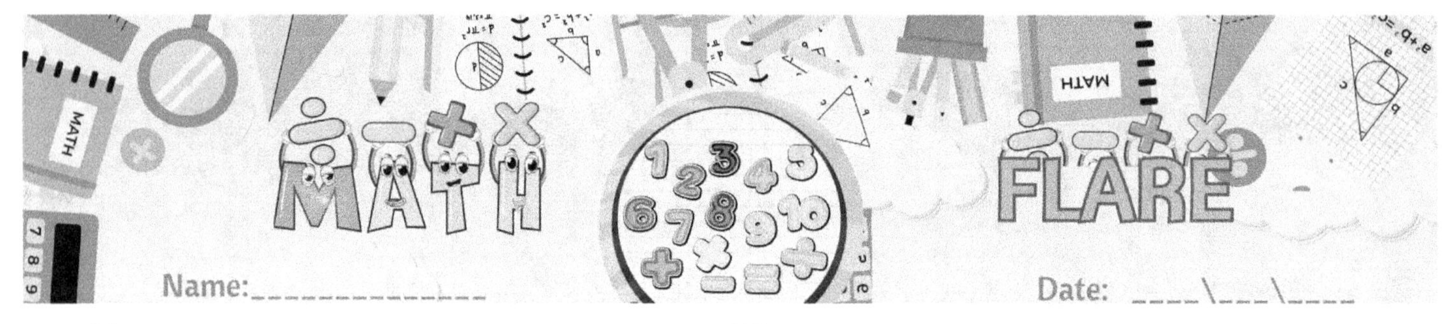

49. $\dfrac{3}{11} + \dfrac{4}{11} =$ _______________

50. $\dfrac{1}{10} + \dfrac{6}{10} =$ _______________

51. $\dfrac{2}{7} + \dfrac{4}{7} =$ _______________

52. $\dfrac{4}{11} + \dfrac{5}{11} =$ _______________

53. $\dfrac{1}{8} + \dfrac{5}{8} =$ _______________

54. $\dfrac{2}{7} + \dfrac{1}{7} =$ _______________

55. $\dfrac{8}{12} + \dfrac{2}{12} =$ _______________

56. $\dfrac{3}{9} + \dfrac{4}{9} =$ _______________

57. $\dfrac{1}{10} + \dfrac{5}{10} =$ _______________

58. $\dfrac{1}{7} + \dfrac{1}{7} =$ _______________

59. $\dfrac{3}{12} + \dfrac{1}{12} =$ _______________

60. $\dfrac{5}{8} + \dfrac{2}{8} =$ _______________

61. $\dfrac{8}{10} + \dfrac{1}{10} =$ _______________

62. $\dfrac{4}{9} + \dfrac{4}{9} =$ _______________

63. $\dfrac{5}{11} + \dfrac{3}{11} =$ _______________

64. $\dfrac{4}{11} + \dfrac{6}{11} =$ _______________

65. $\dfrac{3}{6} + \dfrac{2}{6} =$ _______________

66. $\dfrac{6}{9} + \dfrac{2}{9} =$ _______________

67. $\dfrac{1}{5} + \dfrac{2}{5} =$ _______________

68. $\dfrac{1}{10} + \dfrac{4}{10} =$ _______________

69. $\dfrac{6}{9} + \dfrac{1}{9} =$ _______________

70. $\dfrac{1}{12} + \dfrac{5}{12} =$ _______________

71. $\dfrac{1}{7} + \dfrac{3}{7} =$ _______________

72. $\dfrac{4}{8} + \dfrac{1}{8} =$ _______________

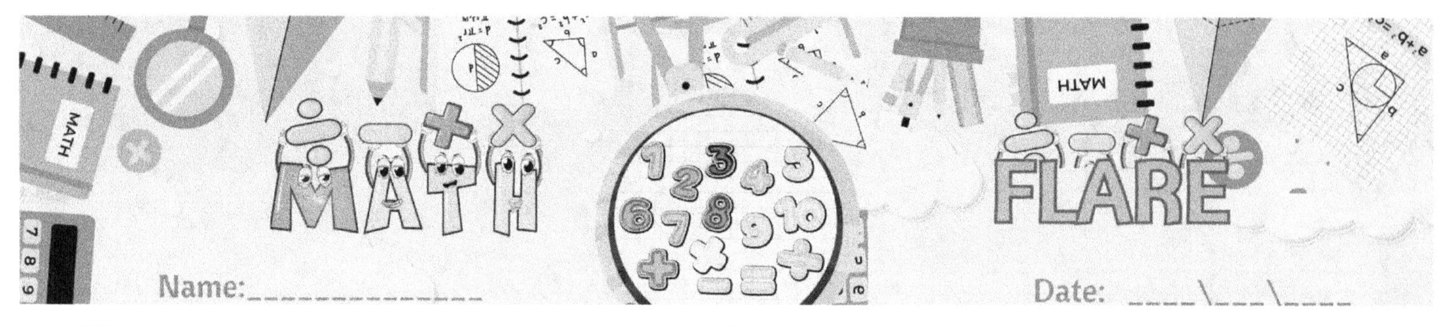

73. $\frac{6}{10} + \frac{2}{10} =$ ___________

74. $\frac{5}{11} + \frac{5}{11} =$ ___________

75. $\frac{2}{4} + \frac{1}{4} =$ ___________

76. $\frac{2}{10} + \frac{6}{10} =$ ___________

77. $\frac{2}{12} + \frac{1}{12} =$ ___________

78. $\frac{8}{11} + \frac{1}{11} =$ ___________

79. $\frac{1}{9} + \frac{1}{9} =$ ___________

80. $\frac{3}{8} + \frac{2}{8} =$ ___________

81. $\frac{1}{7} + \frac{5}{7} =$ ___________

82. $\frac{2}{6} + \frac{1}{6} =$ ___________

83. $\frac{5}{9} + \frac{3}{9} =$ ___________

84. $\frac{3}{11} + \frac{1}{11} =$ ___________

85. $\dfrac{2}{12} + \dfrac{5}{12} =$ _______________

86. $\dfrac{1}{9} + \dfrac{3}{9} =$ _______________

87. $\dfrac{2}{11} + \dfrac{6}{11} =$ _______________

88. $\dfrac{3}{10} + \dfrac{4}{10} =$ _______________

89. $\dfrac{1}{8} + \dfrac{4}{8} =$ _______________

90. $\dfrac{1}{11} + \dfrac{7}{11} =$ _______________

91. $\dfrac{2}{8} + \dfrac{2}{8} =$ _______________

92. $\dfrac{2}{6} + \dfrac{3}{6} =$ _______________

93. $\dfrac{4}{7} + \dfrac{2}{7} =$ _______________

94. $\dfrac{5}{10} + \dfrac{2}{10} =$ _______________

95. $\dfrac{3}{11} + \dfrac{6}{11} =$ _______________

96. $\dfrac{6}{12} + \dfrac{1}{12} =$ _______________

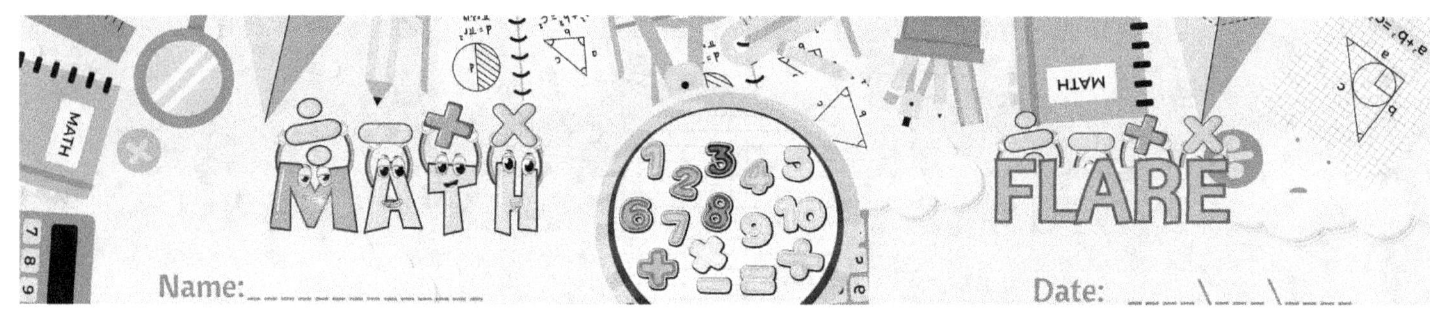

Fractions Subtraction - Common Denominator

Find the difference.

1. $\dfrac{6}{8} - \dfrac{4}{8} =$ _______________

2. $\dfrac{5}{9} - \dfrac{3}{9} =$ _______________

3. $\dfrac{5}{11} - \dfrac{4}{11} =$ _______________

4. $\dfrac{9}{10} - \dfrac{7}{10} =$ _______________

5. $\dfrac{2}{4} - \dfrac{1}{4} =$ _______________

6. $\dfrac{3}{6} - \dfrac{1}{6} =$ _______________

7. $\dfrac{4}{5} - \dfrac{2}{5} =$ _______________

8. $\dfrac{2}{3} - \dfrac{1}{3} =$ _______________

9. $\dfrac{9}{12} - \dfrac{5}{12} =$ _______________

10. $\dfrac{6}{7} - \dfrac{2}{7} =$ _______________

11. $\dfrac{2}{6} - \dfrac{1}{6} =$ _______________

12. $\dfrac{10}{11} - \dfrac{8}{11} =$ _______________

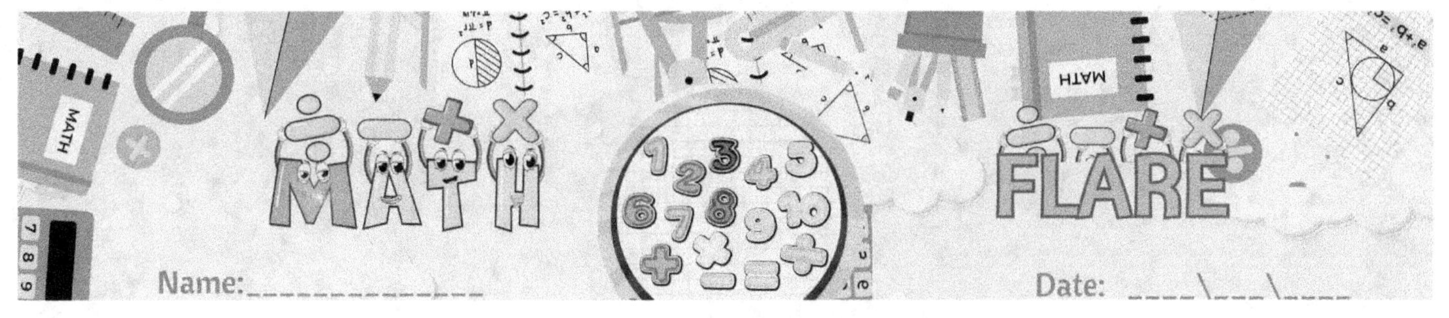

13. $\dfrac{4}{7} - \dfrac{3}{7} =$ _________________

14. $\dfrac{2}{8} - \dfrac{1}{8} =$ _________________

15. $\dfrac{6}{10} - \dfrac{3}{10} =$ _________________

16. $\dfrac{6}{9} - \dfrac{5}{9} =$ _________________

17. $\dfrac{11}{12} - \dfrac{10}{12} =$ _________________

18. $\dfrac{6}{7} - \dfrac{4}{7} =$ _________________

19. $\dfrac{9}{10} - \dfrac{2}{10} =$ _________________

20. $\dfrac{7}{8} - \dfrac{6}{8} =$ _________________

21. $\dfrac{4}{5} - \dfrac{3}{5} =$ _________________

22. $\dfrac{11}{12} - \dfrac{8}{12} =$ _________________

23. $\dfrac{9}{11} - \dfrac{6}{11} =$ _________________

24. $\dfrac{3}{4} - \dfrac{2}{4} =$ _________________

25. $\dfrac{4}{6} - \dfrac{3}{6} =$ _________________

26. $\dfrac{4}{9} - \dfrac{2}{9} =$ _________________

27. $\dfrac{2}{5} - \dfrac{1}{5} =$ _________________

28. $\dfrac{11}{12} - \dfrac{3}{12} =$ _________________

29. $\dfrac{2}{9} - \dfrac{1}{9} =$ _________________

30. $\dfrac{3}{4} - \dfrac{1}{4} =$ _________________

31. $\dfrac{5}{7} - \dfrac{1}{7} =$ _________________

32. $\dfrac{10}{11} - \dfrac{2}{11} =$ _________________

33. $\dfrac{5}{6} - \dfrac{4}{6} =$ _________________

34. $\dfrac{11}{12} - \dfrac{4}{12} =$ _________________

35. $\dfrac{7}{9} - \dfrac{5}{9} =$ _________________

36. $\dfrac{3}{5} - \dfrac{1}{5} =$ _________________

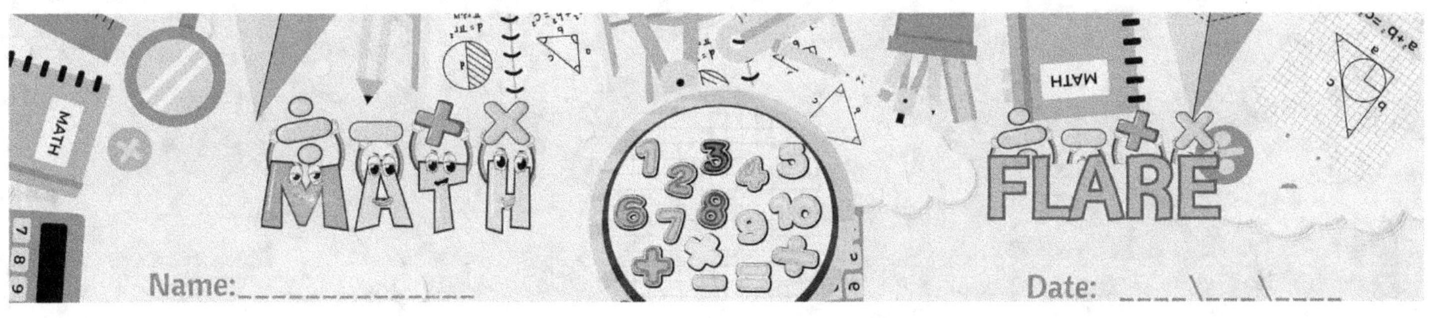

37. $\dfrac{8}{10} - \dfrac{7}{10} =$ _________________

38. $\dfrac{6}{7} - \dfrac{5}{7} =$ _________________

39. $\dfrac{9}{11} - \dfrac{5}{11} =$ _________________

40. $\dfrac{7}{8} - \dfrac{5}{8} =$ _________________

41. $\dfrac{7}{12} - \dfrac{5}{12} =$ _________________

42. $\dfrac{7}{10} - \dfrac{4}{10} =$ _________________

43. $\dfrac{10}{11} - \dfrac{7}{11} =$ _________________

44. $\dfrac{8}{9} - \dfrac{7}{9} =$ _________________

45. $\dfrac{5}{7} - \dfrac{2}{7} =$ _________________

46. $\dfrac{9}{11} - \dfrac{2}{11} =$ _________________

47. $\dfrac{4}{7} - \dfrac{1}{7} =$ _________________

48. $\dfrac{5}{6} - \dfrac{3}{6} =$ _________________

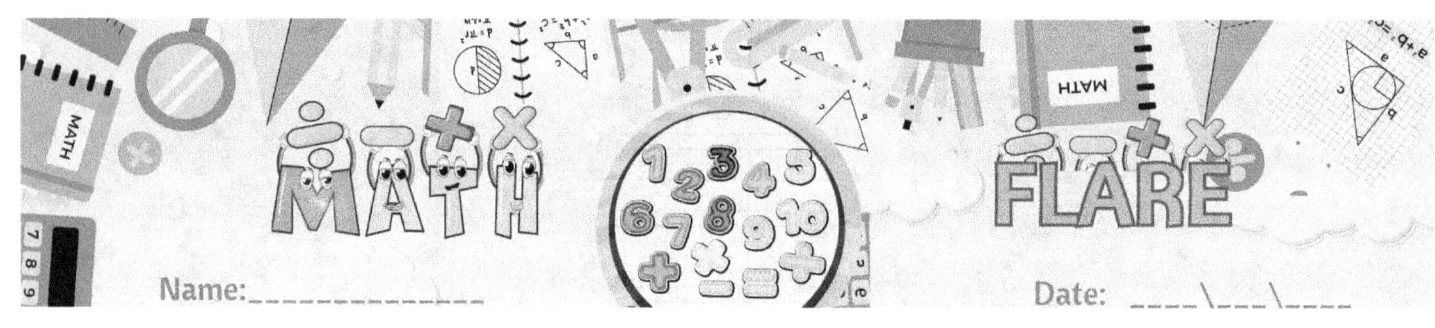

49. $\dfrac{7}{9} - \dfrac{6}{9} =$ _______________

50. $\dfrac{9}{12} - \dfrac{7}{12} =$ _______________

51. $\dfrac{9}{10} - \dfrac{1}{10} =$ _______________

52. $\dfrac{3}{7} - \dfrac{1}{7} =$ _______________

53. $\dfrac{10}{12} - \dfrac{7}{12} =$ _______________

54. $\dfrac{3}{8} - \dfrac{1}{8} =$ _______________

55. $\dfrac{10}{11} - \dfrac{9}{11} =$ _______________

56. $\dfrac{8}{12} - \dfrac{2}{12} =$ _______________

57. $\dfrac{4}{5} - \dfrac{1}{5} =$ _______________

58. $\dfrac{9}{10} - \dfrac{4}{10} =$ _______________

59. $\dfrac{5}{6} - \dfrac{2}{6} =$ _______________

60. $\dfrac{11}{12} - \dfrac{5}{12} =$ _______________

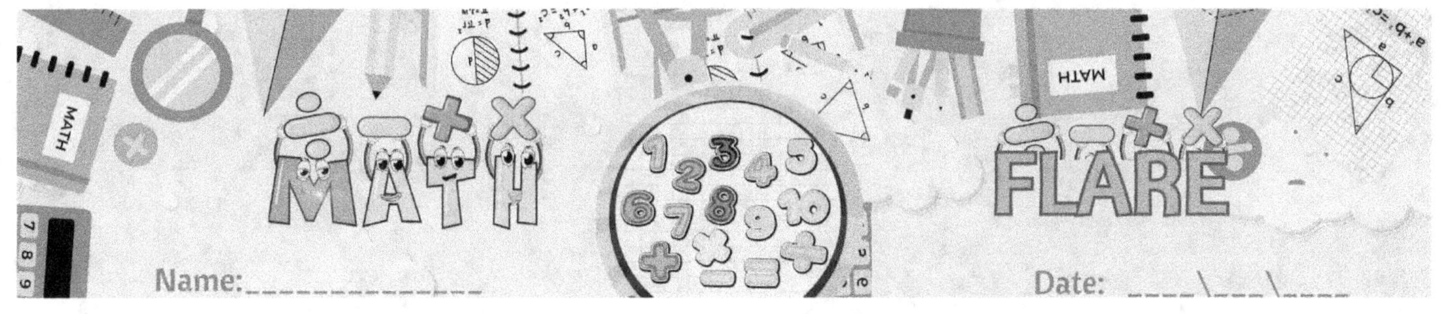

61. $\dfrac{5}{7} - \dfrac{4}{7} =$ _________________

62. $\dfrac{4}{6} - \dfrac{2}{6} =$ _________________

63. $\dfrac{5}{8} - \dfrac{1}{8} =$ _________________

64. $\dfrac{5}{10} - \dfrac{2}{10} =$ _________________

65. $\dfrac{9}{10} - \dfrac{5}{10} =$ _________________

66. $\dfrac{5}{6} - \dfrac{1}{6} =$ _________________

67. $\dfrac{9}{11} - \dfrac{3}{11} =$ _________________

68. $\dfrac{4}{6} - \dfrac{1}{6} =$ _________________

69. $\dfrac{10}{12} - \dfrac{8}{12} =$ _________________

70. $\dfrac{4}{10} - \dfrac{3}{10} =$ _________________

71. $\dfrac{8}{9} - \dfrac{4}{9} =$ _________________

72. $\dfrac{3}{5} - \dfrac{2}{5} =$ _________________

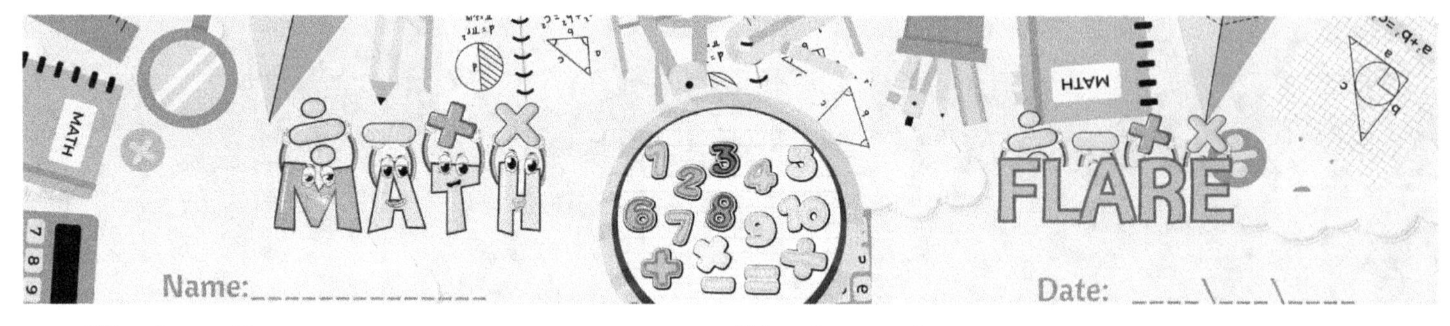

73. $\dfrac{6}{8} - \dfrac{3}{8} =$ _______________

74. $\dfrac{9}{10} - \dfrac{8}{10} =$ _______________

75. $\dfrac{10}{11} - \dfrac{5}{11} =$ _______________

76. $\dfrac{6}{9} - \dfrac{3}{9} =$ _______________

77. $\dfrac{5}{12} - \dfrac{4}{12} =$ _______________

78. $\dfrac{6}{7} - \dfrac{1}{7} =$ _______________

79. $\dfrac{10}{11} - \dfrac{6}{11} =$ _______________

80. $\dfrac{11}{12} - \dfrac{9}{12} =$ _______________

81. $\dfrac{5}{9} - \dfrac{2}{9} =$ _______________

82. $\dfrac{5}{12} - \dfrac{1}{12} =$ _______________

83. $\dfrac{3}{8} - \dfrac{2}{8} =$ _______________

84. $\dfrac{8}{9} - \dfrac{5}{9} =$ _______________

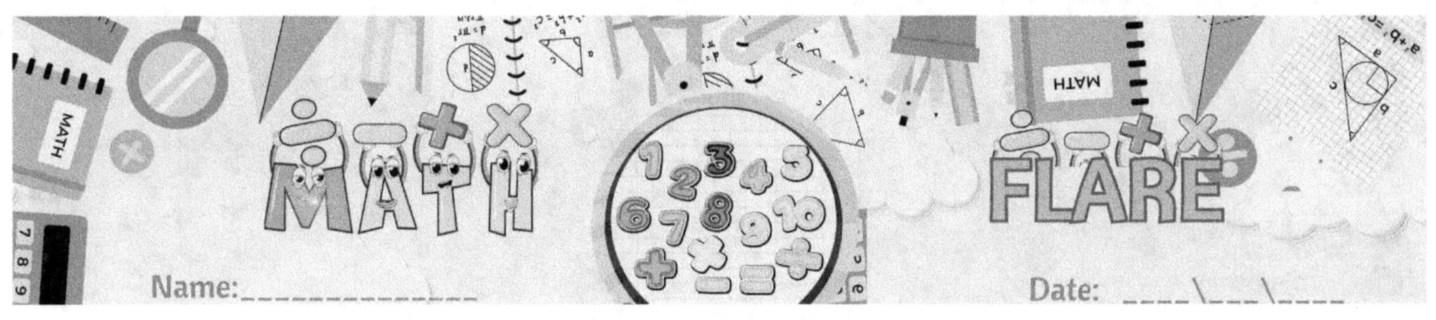

85. $\dfrac{8}{10} - \dfrac{1}{10} =$ _________________

86. $\dfrac{3}{11} - \dfrac{2}{11} =$ _________________

87. $\dfrac{6}{12} - \dfrac{5}{12} =$ _________________

88. $\dfrac{5}{11} - \dfrac{3}{11} =$ _________________

89. $\dfrac{8}{9} - \dfrac{1}{9} =$ _________________

90. $\dfrac{4}{8} - \dfrac{1}{8} =$ _________________

91. $\dfrac{9}{11} - \dfrac{8}{11} =$ _________________

92. $\dfrac{7}{10} - \dfrac{2}{10} =$ _________________

93. $\dfrac{4}{8} - \dfrac{3}{8} =$ _________________

94. $\dfrac{6}{11} - \dfrac{5}{11} =$ _________________

95. $\dfrac{9}{10} - \dfrac{6}{10} =$ _________________

96. $\dfrac{6}{11} - \dfrac{3}{11} =$ _________________

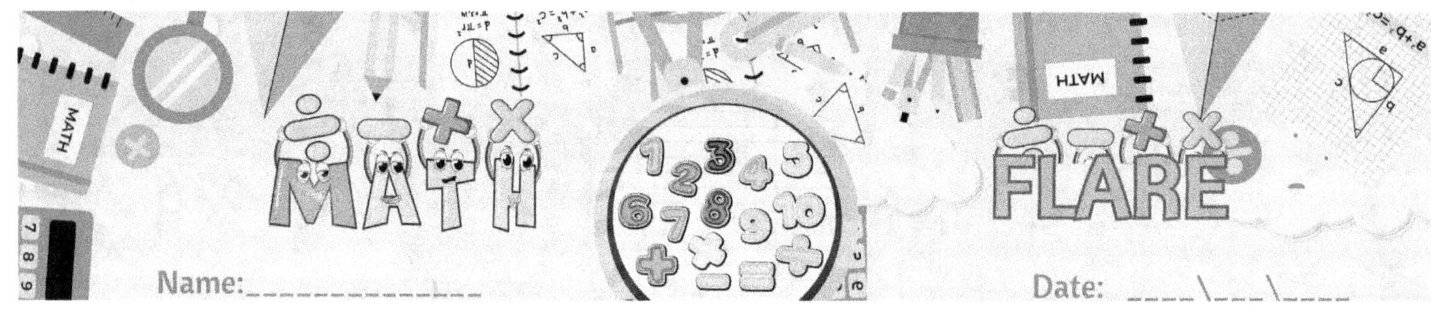

Fractions Multiplication

Find the product.

1. $\dfrac{4}{5} \times \dfrac{3}{7} =$ __________

2. $\dfrac{3}{4} \times \dfrac{5}{6} =$ __________

3. $\dfrac{5}{8} \times \dfrac{4}{5} =$ __________

4. $\dfrac{1}{2} \times \dfrac{3}{7} =$ __________

5. $\dfrac{6}{7} \times \dfrac{1}{2} =$ __________

6. $\dfrac{3}{4} \times \dfrac{2}{9} =$ __________

7. $\dfrac{1}{5} \times \dfrac{1}{4} =$ __________

8. $\dfrac{7}{12} \times \dfrac{2}{3} =$ __________

9. $\dfrac{10}{11} \times \dfrac{2}{5} =$ __________

10. $\dfrac{2}{5} \times \dfrac{8}{11} =$ __________

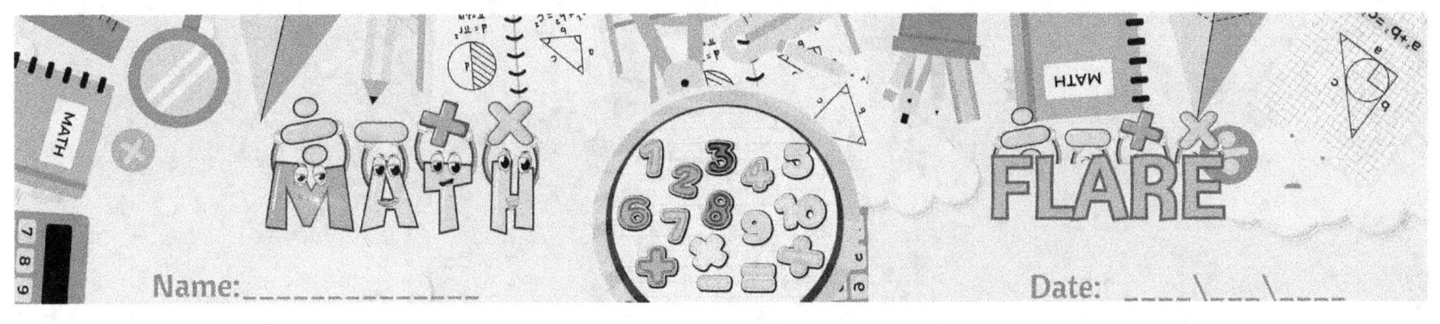

11. $\dfrac{3}{4} \times \dfrac{3}{4} =$ _______________

12. $\dfrac{5}{7} \times \dfrac{1}{2} =$ _______________

13. $\dfrac{1}{2} \times \dfrac{1}{2} =$ _______________

14. $\dfrac{2}{3} \times \dfrac{1}{4} =$ _______________

15. $\dfrac{1}{3} \times \dfrac{1}{3} =$ _______________

16. $\dfrac{1}{2} \times \dfrac{4}{11} =$ _______________

17. $\dfrac{3}{4} \times \dfrac{2}{5} =$ _______________

18. $\dfrac{1}{11} \times \dfrac{5}{12} =$ _______________

19. $\dfrac{7}{12} \times \dfrac{8}{9} =$ _______________

20. $\dfrac{5}{6} \times \dfrac{1}{4} =$ _______________

21. $\dfrac{3}{4} \times \dfrac{4}{7} =$ _______________

22. $\dfrac{1}{2} \times \dfrac{5}{6} =$ _______________

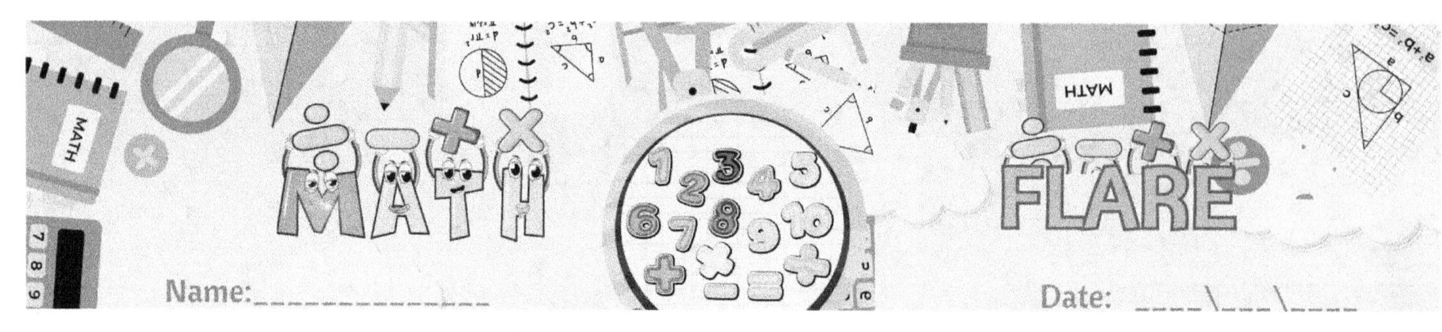

23. $\dfrac{2}{5} \times \dfrac{2}{3} =$ _______________

24. $\dfrac{2}{3} \times \dfrac{1}{3} =$ _______________

25. $\dfrac{1}{2} \times \dfrac{2}{11} =$ _______________

26. $\dfrac{1}{2} \times \dfrac{5}{8} =$ _______________

27. $\dfrac{3}{4} \times \dfrac{3}{5} =$ _______________

28. $\dfrac{3}{5} \times \dfrac{1}{4} =$ _______________

29. $\dfrac{2}{3} \times \dfrac{5}{9} =$ _______________

30. $\dfrac{4}{11} \times \dfrac{1}{5} =$ _______________

31. $\dfrac{1}{4} \times \dfrac{1}{3} =$ _______________

32. $\dfrac{1}{5} \times \dfrac{1}{2} =$ _______________

33. $\dfrac{1}{8} \times \dfrac{3}{5} =$ _______________

34. $\dfrac{1}{3} \times \dfrac{8}{11} =$ _______________

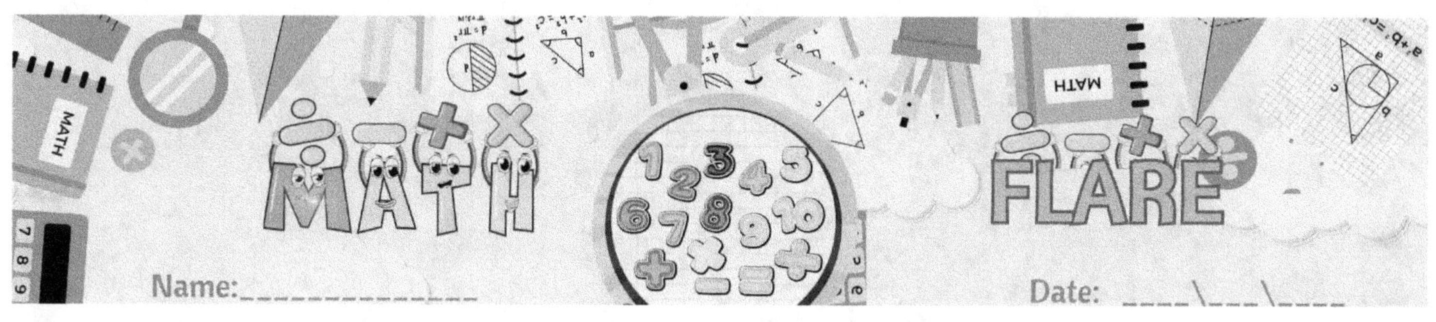

35. $\dfrac{1}{7} \times \dfrac{2}{9} =$ _______________

36. $\dfrac{1}{3} \times \dfrac{6}{7} =$ _______________

37. $\dfrac{1}{2} \times \dfrac{2}{7} =$ _______________

38. $\dfrac{4}{5} \times \dfrac{1}{4} =$ _______________

39. $\dfrac{1}{3} \times \dfrac{2}{3} =$ _______________

40. $\dfrac{5}{6} \times \dfrac{3}{4} =$ _______________

41. $\dfrac{5}{9} \times \dfrac{1}{3} =$ _______________

42. $\dfrac{3}{4} \times \dfrac{1}{2} =$ _______________

43. $\dfrac{4}{5} \times \dfrac{5}{12} =$ _______________

44. $\dfrac{1}{2} \times \dfrac{1}{3} =$ _______________

45. $\dfrac{2}{3} \times \dfrac{1}{10} =$ _______________

46. $\dfrac{1}{2} \times \dfrac{3}{5} =$ _______________

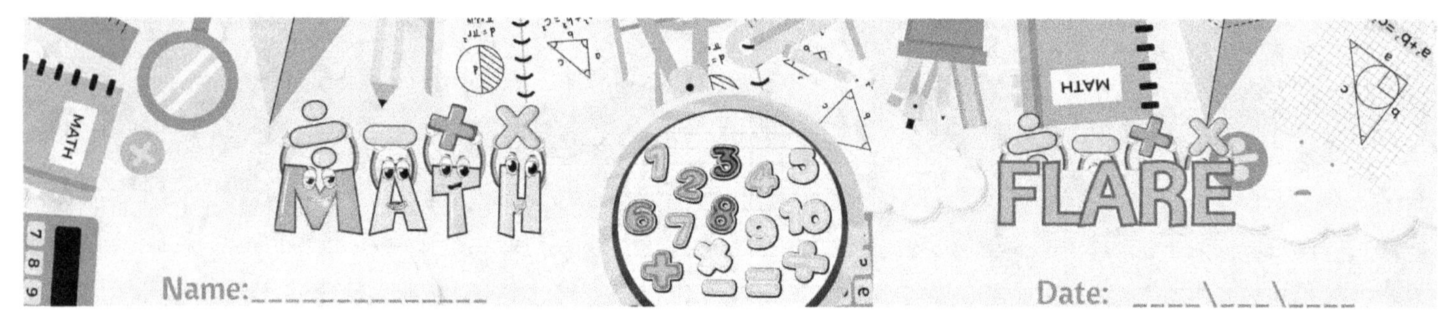

47. $\dfrac{5}{6} \times \dfrac{2}{3} =$ _______________

48. $\dfrac{1}{2} \times \dfrac{10}{11} =$ _______________

49. $\dfrac{2}{3} \times \dfrac{5}{7} =$ _______________

50. $\dfrac{4}{11} \times \dfrac{2}{5} =$ _______________

51. $\dfrac{3}{8} \times \dfrac{3}{10} =$ _______________

52. $\dfrac{1}{4} \times \dfrac{1}{2} =$ _______________

53. $\dfrac{2}{11} \times \dfrac{2}{5} =$ _______________

54. $\dfrac{3}{4} \times \dfrac{4}{11} =$ _______________

55. $\dfrac{7}{9} \times \dfrac{7}{9} =$ _______________

56. $\dfrac{1}{2} \times \dfrac{4}{7} =$ _______________

57. $\dfrac{4}{7} \times \dfrac{1}{2} =$ _______________

58. $\dfrac{3}{8} \times \dfrac{3}{4} =$ _______________

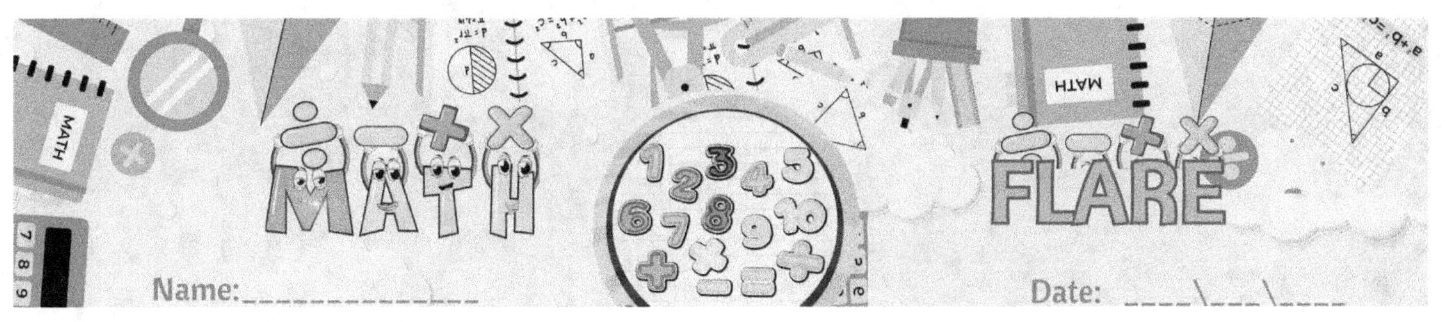

59. $\dfrac{5}{7} \times \dfrac{3}{4} =$ _______________

60. $\dfrac{1}{10} \times \dfrac{1}{6} =$ _______________

61. $\dfrac{11}{12} \times \dfrac{1}{2} =$ _______________

62. $\dfrac{1}{3} \times \dfrac{1}{5} =$ _______________

63. $\dfrac{3}{8} \times \dfrac{5}{6} =$ _______________

64. $\dfrac{4}{9} \times \dfrac{1}{10} =$ _______________

65. $\dfrac{2}{3} \times \dfrac{3}{8} =$ _______________

66. $\dfrac{1}{10} \times \dfrac{1}{5} =$ _______________

67. $\dfrac{1}{8} \times \dfrac{1}{3} =$ _______________

68. $\dfrac{1}{3} \times \dfrac{1}{4} =$ _______________

69. $\dfrac{1}{3} \times \dfrac{2}{5} =$ _______________

70. $\dfrac{1}{5} \times \dfrac{1}{8} =$ _______________

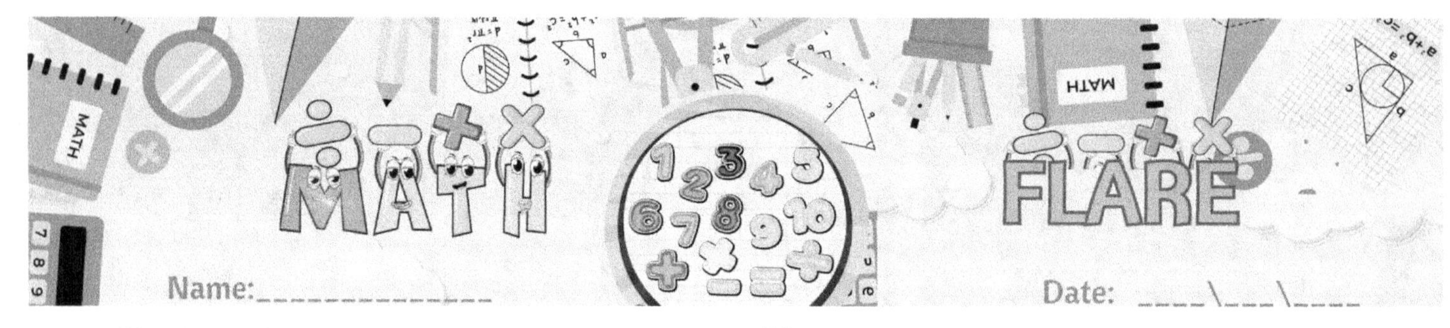

71. $\dfrac{1}{5} \times \dfrac{6}{7} =$ _______________

72. $\dfrac{1}{3} \times \dfrac{3}{5} =$ _______________

73. $\dfrac{1}{4} \times \dfrac{1}{10} =$ _______________

74. $\dfrac{7}{9} \times \dfrac{1}{4} =$ _______________

75. $\dfrac{1}{8} \times \dfrac{1}{2} =$ _______________

76. $\dfrac{2}{3} \times \dfrac{4}{9} =$ _______________

77. $\dfrac{1}{6} \times \dfrac{1}{4} =$ _______________

78. $\dfrac{8}{11} \times \dfrac{7}{8} =$ _______________

79. $\dfrac{1}{2} \times \dfrac{2}{5} =$ _______________

80. $\dfrac{2}{3} \times \dfrac{1}{2} =$ _______________

81. $\dfrac{5}{6} \times \dfrac{1}{3} =$ _______________

82. $\dfrac{1}{2} \times \dfrac{1}{4} =$ _______________

83. $\dfrac{2}{3} \times \dfrac{5}{11} =$ _______________

84. $\dfrac{1}{6} \times \dfrac{1}{3} =$ _______________

85. $\dfrac{3}{7} \times \dfrac{1}{3} =$ _______________

86. $\dfrac{1}{2} \times \dfrac{1}{8} =$ _______________

87. $\dfrac{1}{2} \times \dfrac{2}{3} =$ _______________

88. $\dfrac{4}{9} \times \dfrac{2}{11} =$ _______________

89. $\dfrac{1}{11} \times \dfrac{4}{5} =$ _______________

90. $\dfrac{1}{4} \times \dfrac{4}{9} =$ _______________

91. $\dfrac{1}{2} \times \dfrac{4}{5} =$ _______________

92. $\dfrac{3}{5} \times \dfrac{5}{6} =$ _______________

93. $\dfrac{1}{3} \times \dfrac{3}{4} =$ _______________

94. $\dfrac{4}{9} \times \dfrac{8}{11} =$ _______________

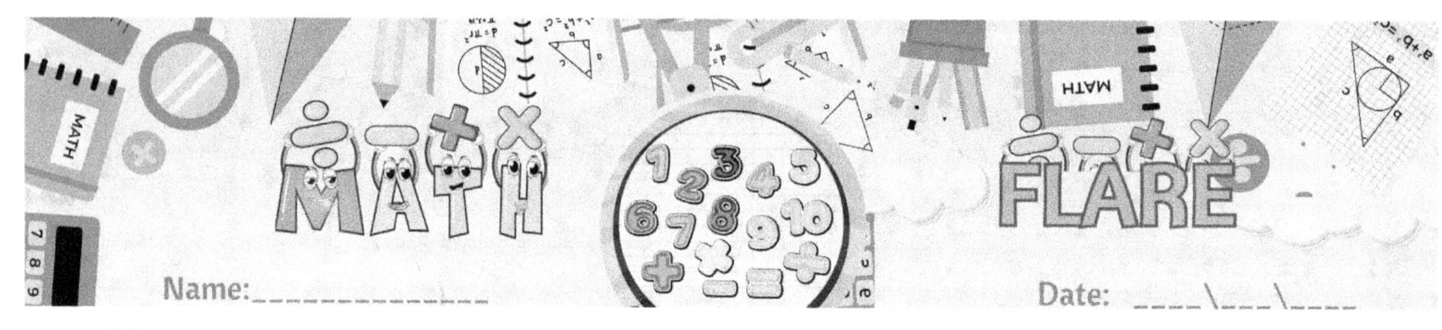

95. $\dfrac{5}{8} \times \dfrac{4}{7} =$ _______________

96. $\dfrac{1}{9} \times \dfrac{2}{3} =$ _______________

97. $\dfrac{1}{5} \times \dfrac{2}{3} =$ _______________

98. $\dfrac{1}{11} \times \dfrac{3}{4} =$ _______________

99. $\dfrac{4}{9} \times \dfrac{5}{8} =$ _______________

100. $\dfrac{4}{5} \times \dfrac{2}{7} =$ _______________

101. $\dfrac{2}{3} \times \dfrac{2}{3} =$ _______________

102. $\dfrac{4}{5} \times \dfrac{2}{5} =$ _______________

103. $\dfrac{2}{7} \times \dfrac{1}{3} =$ _______________

104. $\dfrac{1}{6} \times \dfrac{1}{2} =$ _______________

105. $\dfrac{10}{11} \times \dfrac{1}{5} =$ _______________

106. $\dfrac{3}{7} \times \dfrac{3}{4} =$ _______________

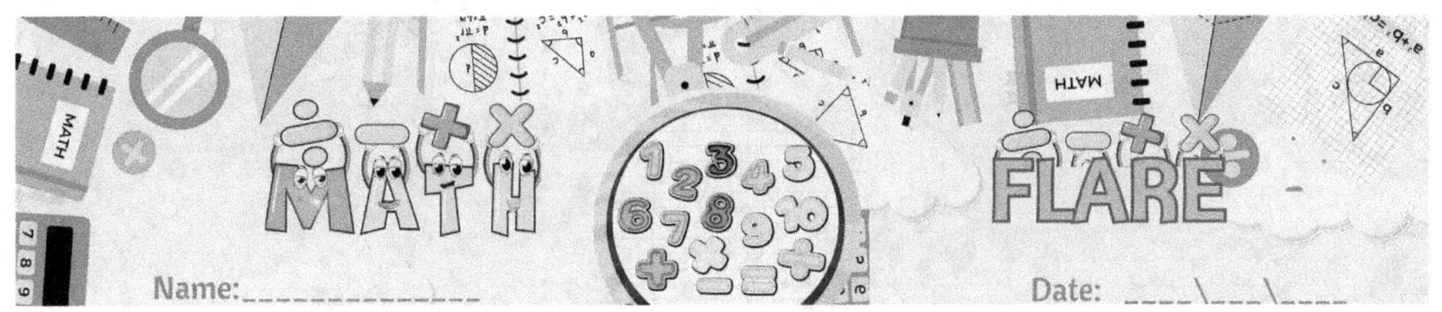

Fractions Division

Find the quotient.

1. $\dfrac{1}{6} \div \dfrac{6}{7} =$ _______________

2. $\dfrac{1}{12} \div \dfrac{4}{8} =$ _______________

3. $\dfrac{4}{9} \div \dfrac{1}{9} =$ _______________

4. $\dfrac{2}{3} \div \dfrac{7}{10} =$ _______________

5. $\dfrac{1}{5} \div \dfrac{1}{2} =$ _______________

6. $\dfrac{1}{2} \div \dfrac{3}{11} =$ _______________

7. $\dfrac{1}{10} \div \dfrac{3}{9} =$ _______________

8. $\dfrac{5}{11} \div \dfrac{9}{10} =$ _______________

9. $\dfrac{6}{7} \div \dfrac{2}{11} =$ _______________

10. $\dfrac{1}{10} \div \dfrac{2}{3} =$ _______________

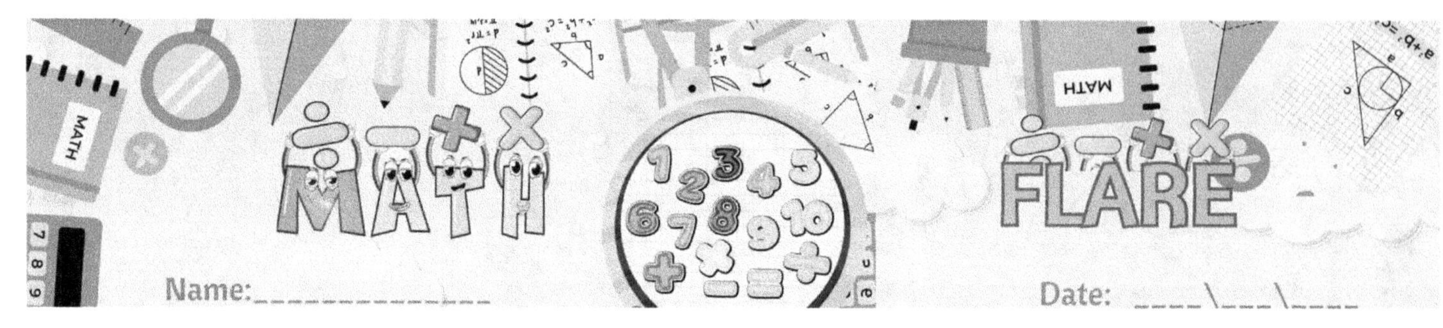

11. $\dfrac{7}{8} \div \dfrac{1}{12} =$ _______________

12. $\dfrac{7}{9} \div \dfrac{3}{4} =$ _______________

13. $\dfrac{2}{5} \div \dfrac{9}{11} =$ _______________

14. $\dfrac{3}{10} \div \dfrac{2}{3} =$ _______________

15. $\dfrac{1}{6} \div \dfrac{6}{12} =$ _______________

16. $\dfrac{6}{7} \div \dfrac{2}{9} =$ _______________

17. $\dfrac{1}{4} \div \dfrac{4}{8} =$ _______________

18. $\dfrac{2}{11} \div \dfrac{2}{4} =$ _______________

19. $\dfrac{3}{8} \div \dfrac{2}{5} =$ _______________

20. $\dfrac{8}{9} \div \dfrac{4}{6} =$ _______________

21. $\dfrac{2}{7} \div \dfrac{1}{3} =$ _______________

22. $\dfrac{3}{10} \div \dfrac{7}{8} =$ _______________

23. $\dfrac{1}{4} \div \dfrac{1}{10} =$ _______________

24. $\dfrac{1}{6} \div \dfrac{1}{2} =$ _______________

25. $\dfrac{4}{5} \div \dfrac{3}{6} =$ _______________

26. $\dfrac{1}{4} \div \dfrac{2}{3} =$ _______________

27. $\dfrac{1}{12} \div \dfrac{6}{8} =$ _______________

28. $\dfrac{10}{11} \div \dfrac{6}{12} =$ _______________

29. $\dfrac{1}{2} \div \dfrac{3}{7} =$ _______________

30. $\dfrac{1}{4} \div \dfrac{5}{10} =$ _______________

31. $\dfrac{3}{7} \div \dfrac{3}{5} =$ _______________

32. $\dfrac{3}{10} \div \dfrac{4}{8} =$ _______________

33. $\dfrac{1}{2} \div \dfrac{1}{3} =$ _______________

34. $\dfrac{1}{6} \div \dfrac{5}{9} =$ _______________

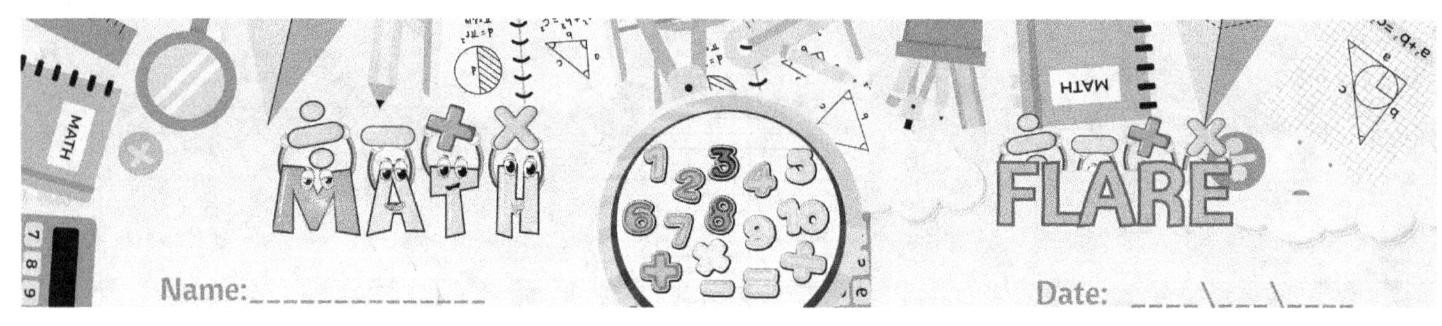

35. $\dfrac{1}{8} \div \dfrac{1}{4} =$ _______________

36. $\dfrac{3}{10} \div \dfrac{5}{10} =$ _______________

37. $\dfrac{2}{11} \div \dfrac{2}{7} =$ _______________

38. $\dfrac{2}{7} \div \dfrac{7}{11} =$ _______________

39. $\dfrac{1}{2} \div \dfrac{5}{6} =$ _______________

40. $\dfrac{5}{9} \div \dfrac{2}{7} =$ _______________

41. $\dfrac{7}{9} \div \dfrac{2}{3} =$ _______________

42. $\dfrac{1}{8} \div \dfrac{3}{5} =$ _______________

43. $\dfrac{2}{3} \div \dfrac{1}{2} =$ _______________

44. $\dfrac{1}{4} \div \dfrac{9}{12} =$ _______________

45. $\dfrac{3}{5} \div \dfrac{6}{9} =$ _______________

46. $\dfrac{1}{3} \div \dfrac{1}{12} =$ _______________

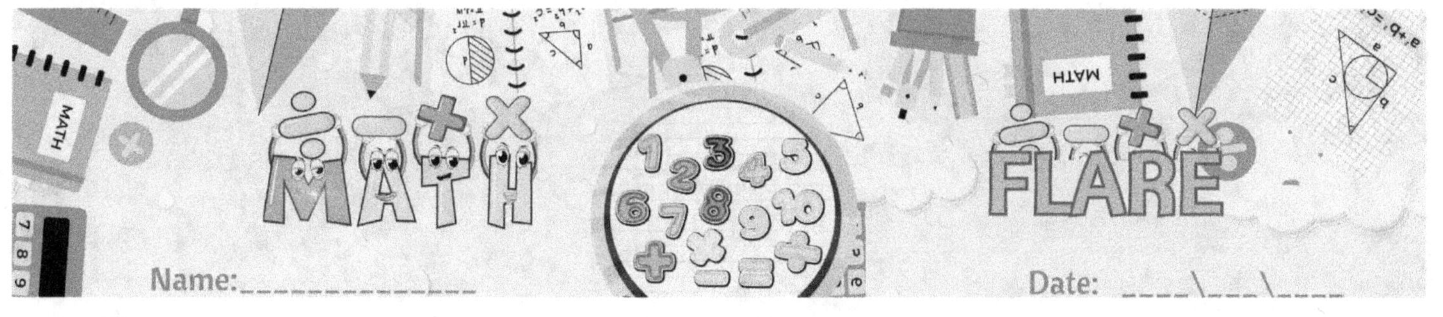

47. $\dfrac{1}{4} \div \dfrac{2}{5} =$ ___________________

48. $\dfrac{1}{2} \div \dfrac{1}{2} =$ ___________________

49. $\dfrac{3}{5} \div \dfrac{8}{10} =$ ___________________

50. $\dfrac{1}{3} \div \dfrac{6}{8} =$ ___________________

51. $\dfrac{3}{7} \div \dfrac{4}{9} =$ ___________________

52. $\dfrac{2}{3} \div \dfrac{6}{9} =$ ___________________

53. $\dfrac{9}{10} \div \dfrac{1}{11} =$ ___________________

54. $\dfrac{4}{7} \div \dfrac{8}{10} =$ ___________________

55. $\dfrac{3}{5} \div \dfrac{1}{5} =$ ___________________

56. $\dfrac{1}{2} \div \dfrac{1}{8} =$ ___________________

57. $\dfrac{1}{6} \div \dfrac{11}{12} =$ ___________________

58. $\dfrac{1}{2} \div \dfrac{6}{8} =$ ___________________

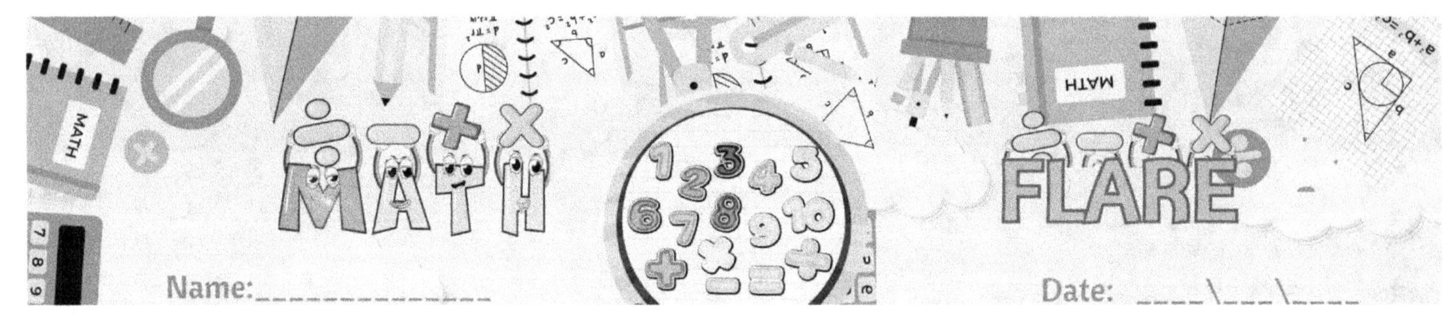

59. $\dfrac{1}{6} \div \dfrac{5}{7} =$ _________________

60. $\dfrac{4}{7} \div \dfrac{1}{2} =$ _________________

61. $\dfrac{1}{3} \div \dfrac{3}{4} =$ _________________

62. $\dfrac{1}{12} \div \dfrac{2}{5} =$ _________________

63. $\dfrac{2}{3} \div \dfrac{3}{6} =$ _________________

64. $\dfrac{2}{9} \div \dfrac{6}{8} =$ _________________

65. $\dfrac{4}{5} \div \dfrac{3}{4} =$ _________________

66. $\dfrac{10}{11} \div \dfrac{7}{9} =$ _________________

67. $\dfrac{1}{6} \div \dfrac{10}{12} =$ _________________

68. $\dfrac{7}{12} \div \dfrac{1}{2} =$ _________________

69. $\dfrac{1}{7} \div \dfrac{2}{4} =$ _________________

70. $\dfrac{5}{6} \div \dfrac{2}{3} =$ _________________

71. $\dfrac{1}{3} \div \dfrac{2}{10} =$ _______________

72. $\dfrac{3}{4} \div \dfrac{3}{11} =$ _______________

73. $\dfrac{3}{8} \div \dfrac{4}{12} =$ _______________

74. $\dfrac{7}{10} \div \dfrac{4}{8} =$ _______________

75. $\dfrac{4}{5} \div \dfrac{1}{6} =$ _______________

76. $\dfrac{1}{4} \div \dfrac{1}{2} =$ _______________

77. $\dfrac{1}{2} \div \dfrac{4}{10} =$ _______________

78. $\dfrac{7}{8} \div \dfrac{4}{11} =$ _______________

79. $\dfrac{1}{2} \div \dfrac{3}{4} =$ _______________

80. $\dfrac{7}{12} \div \dfrac{2}{3} =$ _______________

81. $\dfrac{1}{4} \div \dfrac{7}{8} =$ _______________

82. $\dfrac{3}{10} \div \dfrac{7}{9} =$ _______________

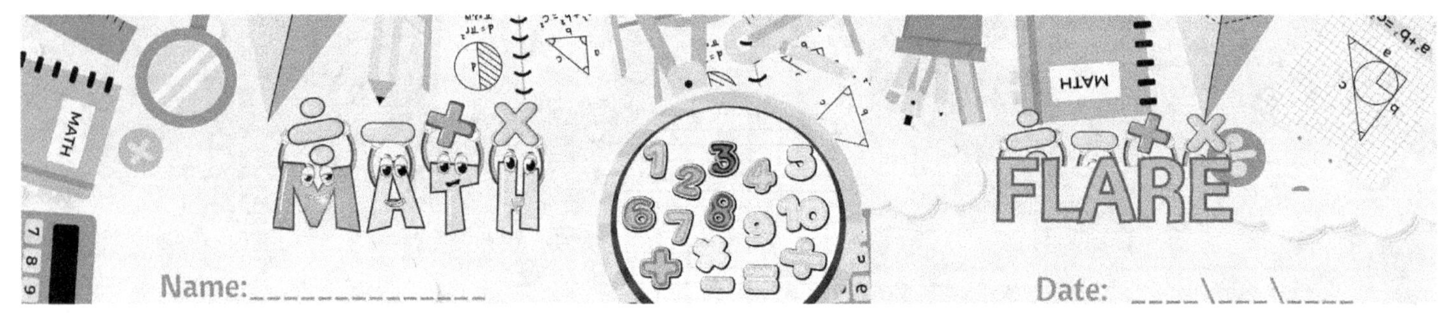

83. $\dfrac{1}{7} \div \dfrac{3}{7} =$ ___________________

84. $\dfrac{5}{9} \div \dfrac{2}{11} =$ ___________________

85. $\dfrac{1}{3} \div \dfrac{1}{4} =$ ___________________

86. $\dfrac{1}{6} \div \dfrac{3}{5} =$ ___________________

87. $\dfrac{6}{11} \div \dfrac{2}{3} =$ ___________________

88. $\dfrac{1}{6} \div \dfrac{9}{11} =$ ___________________

89. $\dfrac{1}{4} \div \dfrac{4}{10} =$ ___________________

90. $\dfrac{7}{10} \div \dfrac{7}{8} =$ ___________________

91. $\dfrac{2}{3} \div \dfrac{2}{5} =$ ___________________

92. $\dfrac{3}{8} \div \dfrac{1}{6} =$ ___________________

93. $\dfrac{7}{12} \div \dfrac{6}{10} =$ ___________________

94. $\dfrac{1}{9} \div \dfrac{6}{11} =$ ___________________

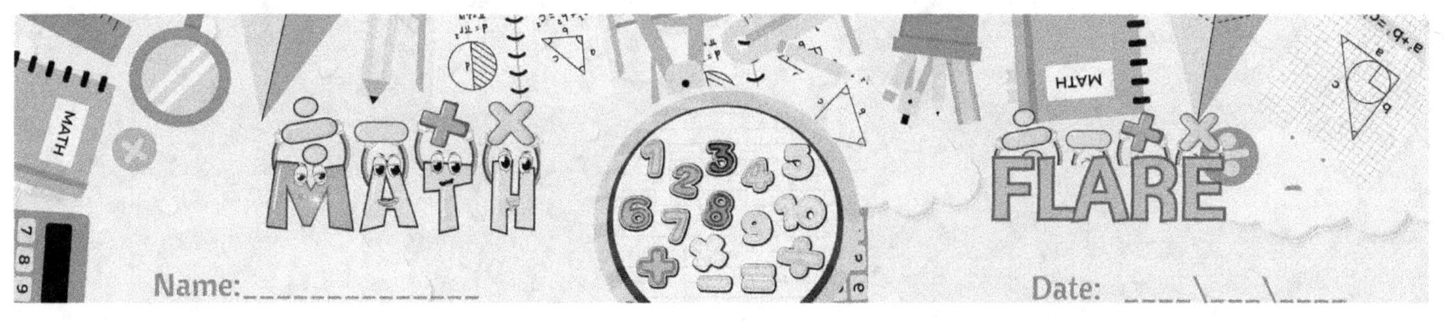

95. $\dfrac{2}{5} \div \dfrac{2}{6} =$ _________________

96. $\dfrac{1}{2} \div \dfrac{11}{12} =$ _________________

97. $\dfrac{2}{7} \div \dfrac{2}{7} =$ _________________

98. $\dfrac{3}{4} \div \dfrac{3}{4} =$ _________________

99. $\dfrac{2}{11} \div \dfrac{3}{5} =$ _________________

100. $\dfrac{1}{8} \div \dfrac{3}{12} =$ _________________

101. $\dfrac{3}{4} \div \dfrac{2}{5} =$ _________________

102. $\dfrac{2}{3} \div \dfrac{3}{7} =$ _________________

103. $\dfrac{1}{6} \div \dfrac{3}{8} =$ _________________

104. $\dfrac{1}{2} \div \dfrac{1}{6} =$ _________________

105. $\dfrac{1}{12} \div \dfrac{1}{2} =$ _________________

106. $\dfrac{2}{3} \div \dfrac{1}{5} =$ _________________

ANSWERS

Page 1:   Fraction Identification

1. 1/2	2. 7/9	3. 1/4	4. 1/2	5. 1/8	6. 2/3
7. 1/2	8. 2/5	9. 1/3	10. 3/5	11. 5/7	12. 1/16
13. 1/10	14. 1/12	15. 3/8	16. 7/15	17. 4/7	18. 2/3
19. 2/3	20. 5/6	21. 1/2	22. 1/3	23. 4/5	24. 1/9
25. 1/2	26. 1/5	27. 3/4	28. 3/4	29. 3/5	30. 4/5
31. 1/4	32. 2/5	33. 1/4	34. 5/9	35. 3/10	36. 7/8
37. 1/2	38. 5/6	39. 1/6	40. 9/10	41. 1/5	42. 13/16
43. 3/7	44. 1/7	45. 13/15	46. 3/16	47. 1/4	48. 1/2
49. 5/8	50. 3/5	51. 2/3	52. 4/5	53. 1/3	54. 11/12
55. 3/4	56. 11/16	57. 14/15	58. 2/5	59. 5/16	60. 1/6
61. 8/9	62. 2/3	63. 2/15	64. 3/8	65. 4/15	66. 1/3
67. 6/7	68. 1/8	69. 8/15	70. 2/9	71. 7/8	72. 5/8
73. 2/7	74. 4/9	75. 1/5	76. 7/16	77. 5/12	78. 11/15
79. 7/10					

Page 11:   Compare the Fractions

1. >	2. =	3. >	4. >	5. <	6. >	7. >	8. <	9. <	10. >
11. <	12. >	13. <	14. >	15. =	16. >	17. >	18. <	19. >	20. >
21. >	22. >	23. <	24. <	25. <	26. >	27. >	28. >	29. >	30. >
31. <	32. <	33. >	34. =	35. >	36. >	37. =	38. >	39. >	40. >

41. <   42. <   43. >   44. <   45. >   46. <   47. <   48. <   49. <   50. >

51. <   52. <   53. <   54. <   55. <   56. <   57. <   58. <   59. >   60. <

61. >   62. >   63. <   64. >   65. <   66. <   67. <   68. >   69. >   70. =

71. >   72. <   73. <   74. >   75. >   76. =   77. >   78. <   79. <   80. >

81. >   82. <   83. <   84. >   85. <   86. <   87. >   88. <   89. >   90. <

91. <   92. <   93. >   94. <   95. >   96. >

Page 19:   Equivalent Fractions

1. 7   2. 9   3. 8   4. 6   5. 17   6. 98   7. 80

8. 27   9. 4   10. 20   11. 15   12. 15   13. 72   14. 4

15. 4   16. 14   17. 16   18. 7   19. 40   20. 2   21. 80

22. 112   23. 50   24. 13   25. 9   26. 7   27. 44   28. 14

29. 60   30. 21   31. 200   32. 2   33. 16   34. 24   35. 30

36. 17   37. 6   38. 32   39. 4   40. 114   41. 15   42. 90

43. 11   44. 6   45. 1   46. 2   47. 16   48. 51   49. 36

50. 10   51. 32   52. 14   53. 9   54. 11   55. 8   56. 9

57. 18   58. 7   59. 55   60. 50   61. 100   62. 24   63. 112

64. 1   65. 5   66. 13   67. 9   68. 4   69. 7   70. 15

71. 6   72. 100   73. 5   74. 102   75. 20   76. 5   77. 4

78. 72   79. 13   80. 2   81. 8   82. 2   83. 14   84. 15

85. 130   86. 2   87. 3   88. 18   89. 80   90. 13   91. 1

92. 12   93. 19   94. 10   95. 4   96. 9   97. 40   98. 9

99. 44   100. 16   101. 20   102. 2   103. 17   104. 4

Page 28:   Fractions Addition: Common Denominator

1. 2/3   2. 2/3   3. 3/4   4. 4/5   5. 3/4   6. 6/11

7. 2/3   8. 5/8   9. 3/7   10. 9/10   11. 8/11   12. 5/6

13. 7/9   14. 1/1   15. 4/5   16. 1/2   17. 5/6   18. 2/5

19. 11/12   20. 4/7   21. 4/5   22. 10/11   23. 1/2   24. 5/7

25. 3/4   26. 5/12   27. 9/11   28. 7/9   29. 3/5   30. 4/5

31. 9/11   32. 1/2   33. 1/2   34. 3/4   35. 6/7   36. 5/6

37. 2/3   38. 5/7   39. 3/5   40. 3/8   41. 5/11   42. 5/6

43. 4/5   44. 2/3   45. 7/9   46. 2/3   47. 7/10   48. 6/11

49. 7/11   50. 7/10   51. 6/7   52. 9/11   53. 3/4   54. 3/7

55. 5/6   56. 7/9   57. 3/5   58. 2/7   59. 1/3   60. 7/8

61. 9/10   62. 8/9   63. 8/11   64. 10/11   65. 5/6   66. 8/9

67. 3/5   68. 1/2   69. 7/9   70. 1/2   71. 4/7   72. 5/8

73. 4/5   74. 10/11   75. 3/4   76. 4/5   77. 1/4   78. 9/11

79. 2/9   80. 5/8   81. 6/7   82. 1/2   83. 8/9   84. 4/11

85. 7/12   86. 4/9   87. 8/11   88. 7/10   89. 5/8   90. 8/11

91. 1/2   92. 5/6   93. 6/7   94. 7/10   95. 9/11   96. 7/12

Page 36:   Fractions Subtraction - Common Denominator

1. 1/4   2. 2/9   3. 1/11   4. 1/5   5. 1/4   6. 1/3   7. 2/5

8. 1/3   9. 1/3   10. 4/7   11. 1/6   12. 2/11   13. 1/7   14. 1/8

15. 3/10   16. 1/9   17. 1/12   18. 2/7   19. 7/10   20. 1/8   21. 1/5

22. 1/4   23. 3/11   24. 1/4   25. 1/6   26. 2/9   27. 1/5   28. 2/3

29. 1/9   30. 1/2   31. 4/7   32. 8/11   33. 1/6   34. 7/12   35. 2/9

36. 2/5   37. 1/10   38. 1/7   39. 4/11   40. 1/4   41. 1/6   42. 3/10

43. 3/11   44. 1/9   45. 3/7   46. 7/11   47. 3/7   48. 1/3   49. 1/9

50. 1/6   51. 4/5   52. 2/7   53. 1/4   54. 1/4   55. 1/11   56. 1/2

57. 3/5   58. 1/2   59. 1/2   60. 1/2   61. 1/7   62. 1/3   63. 1/2

64. 3/10   65. 2/5   66. 2/3   67. 6/11   68. 1/2   69. 1/6   70. 1/10

71. 4/9   72. 1/5   73. 3/8   74. 1/10   75. 5/11   76. 1/3   77. 1/12

78. 5/7   79. 4/11   80. 1/6   81. 1/3   82. 1/3   83. 1/8   84. 1/3

85. 7/10   86. 1/11   87. 1/12   88. 2/11   89. 7/9   90. 3/8   91. 1/11

92. 1/2   93. 1/8   94. 1/11   95. 3/10   96. 3/11

Page 44: Fractions Multiplication

1. 12/35   2. 5/8   3. 1/2   4. 3/14   5. 3/7   6. 1/6

7. 1/20   8. 7/18   9. 4/11   10. 16/55   11. 9/16   12. 5/14

13. 1/4   14. 1/6   15. 1/9   16. 2/11   17. 3/10   18. 5/132

19. 14/27   20. 5/24   21. 3/7   22. 5/12   23. 4/15   24. 2/9

25. 1/11   26. 5/16   27. 9/20   28. 3/20   29. 10/27   30. 4/55

31. 1/12   32. 1/10   33. 3/40   34. 8/33   35. 2/63   36. 2/7

37. 1/7   38. 1/5   39. 2/9   40. 5/8   41. 5/27   42. 3/8

43. 1/3   44. 1/6   45. 1/15   46. 3/10   47. 5/9   48. 5/11

49. 10/21   50. 8/55   51. 9/80   52. 1/8   53. 4/55   54. 3/11

55. 49/81   56. 2/7   57. 2/7   58. 9/32   59. 15/28   60. 1/60

61. 11/24   62. 1/15   63. 5/16   64. 2/45   65. 1/4   66. 1/50

67. 1/24   68. 1/12   69. 2/15   70. 1/40   71. 6/35   72. 1/5

73. 1/40   74. 7/36   75. 1/16   76. 8/27   77. 1/24   78. 7/11

79. 1/5   80. 1/3   81. 5/18   82. 1/8   83. 10/33   84. 1/18

85. 1/7   86. 1/16   87. 1/3   88. 8/99   89. 4/55   90. 1/9

91. 2/5   92. 1/2   93. 1/4   94. 32/99   95. 5/14   96. 2/27

97. 2/15   98. 3/44   99. 5/18   100. 8/35   101. 4/9   102. 8/25

103. 2/21   104. 1/12   105. 2/11   106. 9/28

Page 53: Fractions Division

1. 7/36   2. 1/6   3. 4   4. 20/21   5. 2/5

6. 1 5/6   7. 3/10   8. 50/99   9. 4 5/7   10. 3/20

11. 10 1/2   12. 1 1/27   13. 22/45   14. 9/20   15. 1/3

16. 3 6/7   17. 1/2   18. 4/11   19. 15/16   20. 1 1/3

21. 6/7   22. 12/35   23. 2 1/2   24. 1/3   25. 1 3/5

26. 3/8   27. 1/9   28. 1 9/11   29. 1 1/6   30. 1/2

31. 5/7   32. 3/5   33. 1 1/2   34. 3/10   35. 1/2

36. 3/5   37. 7/11   38. 22/49   39. 3/5   40. 1 17/18

41. 1 1/6   42. 5/24   43. 1 1/3   44. 1/3   45. 9/10

46. 4   47. 5/8   48. 1   49. 3/4   50. 4/9

51. 27/28   52. 1   53. 9 9/10   54. 5/7   55. 3

56. 4   57. 2/11   58. 2/3   59. 7/30   60. 1 1/7

61. 4/9   62. 5/24   63. 1 1/3   64. 8/27   65. 1 1/15

66. 1 13/77   67. 1/5   68. 1 1/6   69. 2/7   70. 1 1/4

71. 1 2/3   72. 2 3/4   73. 1 1/8   74. 1 2/5   75. 4 4/5

76. 1/2   77. 1 1/4   78. 2 13/32   79. 2/3   80. 7/8

81. 2/7   82. 27/70   83. 1/3   84. 3 1/18   85. 1 1/3

86. 5/18   87. 9/11   88. 11/54   89. 5/8   90. 4/5

91. 1 2/3   92. 2 1/4   93. 35/36   94. 11/54   95. 1 1/5

96. 6/11   97. 1   98. 1   99. 10/33   100. 1/2

101. 1 7/8   102. 1 5/9   103. 4/9   104. 3   105. 1/6

106. 3 1/3